# World-Wide Webb

Pauline Webb has unquestionably been one of the most influential women in the Church at home and overseas in the modern era, and is certainly Methodism's most famous daughter.

She was Vice-Moderator of the World Council of Churches from 1968 to 1975, and the first female organizer of religious broadcasting for the BBC World Service, and a familiar voice for many listeners to *Thought for the Day* and *Pause for Thought.*

Pauline Webb lives in London.

# World-Wide Webb

Pauline Webb

CANTERBURY
PRESS
Norwich

First published in 2006 by the Canterbury Press Norwich
(a publishing imprint of Hymns Ancient & Modern Limited,
a registered charity)
9–17 St Alban's Place, London N1 0NX

www.scm-canterburypress.co.uk

British Library Cataloguing in Publication data

A catalogue record for this book is available
from the British Library

ISBN 1–85311–756–0/978–1–85311–756–5

Typeset by Regent Typesetting, London
Printed and bound by
MPG Books Ltd, Bodmin, Cornwall

# Contents

# *Acknowledgments*

My thanks are due to Giles Semper and Colin Morris, who first persuaded me to record my memoirs of a life in which I have travelled for over half a century in all six continents as film-maker, editor, ecumenist and broadcaster. I am grateful to my sister Joy Webb who made my task easier by having faithfully kept so many of my letters home in the days long before there were e-mails. I also thank my 'second family' Robert and Shirley Maginley and my neighbours Renee Linder and Margaret Kirk for the support and sustenance they have given me throughout the long months while I was writing this book. Brigette Bennett spent hours at the Newspaper Library researching significant headlines. Anthony Rendell, BBC World Service Editor, checked my memories of enjoyable years I spent at Bush House, and colleagues at the World Council of Churches in Geneva have been most helpful in supplying relevant documents regarding ecumenical meetings. I am particularly grateful to Dr Mary Tanner, a newly elected World President of the World Council of Churches, for agreeing to write the Foreword.

To all my friends in all parts of the world who have shared in the events recorded here I would say in the words of my namesake St Paul: 'I thank my God upon every remembrance of you, for your fellowship in the gospel from the first day until now'.

# Foreword

Pauline Webb has been for me, as for many others, a role model and inspiration. These pages of her life story show just why that was so. Pauline was way ahead of most women of her generation, indeed is way ahead of most of us still. From her days at university she was open to new adventures, new thoughts, new experiences and yet she was always down to earth, which made it possible for some of us to take seriously what she was saying and to follow her.

The book shows Pauline as a pioneer and leader in the Methodist Church, where she championed the cause of the laity – laywomen and laymen – convinced that partnership of women and men, as well as of lay and ordained, was crucial for the mission of the Church. Her campaigning for the ordination of women began early, and she recalls the speech she made in 1959 to the Methodist Conference at a time when most of us had hardly dared to think that thought.

Pauline was a pioneer too in the ecumenical movement: the first woman to be Vice Moderator of the Central Committee, one of many firsts. Not afraid of controversy, she was a leader in the Programme to Combat Racism, facing up to Malcolm Muggeridge in a hard-hitting television interview and bravely defending the cause in a debate in the Oxford Union. Her championing of the fight against apartheid meant she was banned from entering South Africa and was under surveillance. Pauline was in the forefront of the fight against sexism, co-moderating the conference 'Sexism in the Seventies', which led to the study on the Community of Women and Men in the Church, which was to have a lasting effect on the lives of many women around the world and which presented the churches with a chance to change and be changed. It was appropriate that Pauline should have been invited to preach the sermon at the culmination of the world study, a memorable sermon on the women coming to the tomb on the first Easter morning. At the Vancouver Assembly she again preached a remarkable sermon in which she dared to speak of the experience of women in a way which some found startling, even shocking.

The book is punctuated by accounts of five Assemblies of the World Council, which show a major shift of emphasis in the ecumenical movement, from the unity of the Church to a wider vision of the unity of the Church inextricably related to the unity of human community, with concerns to overcome racism, sexism, violence, and to enable the gradual opening up of a dialogue with those of other faiths. Here is not just an account of Pauline's involvement in all of this, but a valuable reflection on the course of the ecumenical movement.

As if leading in her own church and in the ecumenical movement were not enough, Pauline's career in the media, taken up in her fifties, became a way in which she could use her worldwide experience in the service of broadcasting. She was a natural in a career that until then had been almost entirely the preserve of men. She had the ability to respond to situations around the world as they unfolded, whether some natural disaster or some dramatic world event, bringing the gospel message to bear on the situation. She was the first woman to be appointed as the Organizer of Religious Broadcasting Overseas, indeed the first layperson and the first non-Anglican. How she is missed as a regular contributor to *Thought for the Day* and the *Daily Service*.

In the Methodist Church, in the ecumenical movement, and

in broadcasting, Pauline demonstrated, in a confident yet not threatening or strident way, that women could take responsibility and lead in situations that had hitherto been the domains of men. She never colluded with the systems but contributed with integrity in her compelling and convincing way, using women's experience, and opening up new opportunities for the women who followed her.

The book is something of a travelogue as we are taken from New Zealand to Bangkok, from Russia to South Africa, from the Caribbean to Istanbul. 'Join the ecumenical movement and see the world' was certainly true for Pauline as she travelled to meetings and made visits representing the Council, building the network of friendship that is the essential soil in which unity grows. But for her it was not simply a matter of joining the ecumenical movement and *seeing* the world. Pauline was never simply an onlooker. Wherever she went she had a remarkable capacity for listening and responding to different Christian traditions, different cultural contexts, while exhibiting a particular empathy for those who suffered – the poor, the marginalized, the oppressed, always sensitive to the needs of women and children and the rights of indigenous peoples. All of this experience was to play its part in her career in broadcasting, where she could use the contacts she had made and the understanding of the different countries and cultures she had gained.

This book is more than the story of Pauline Webb, more than a travelogue. It takes us through the major events of the second half of the twentieth century: the rivers of blood speech of Enoch Powell, the assassinations of Martin Luther King and Robert Kennedy, the defeat of apartheid, the collapse of communism, the release from prison of Nelson Mandela, the Gulf War and most recently the invasion of Iraq.

Throughout the telling of her story and the amazing experiences she has had, Pauline comes across not as a remote jet-setter, but as someone rooted in her family life, close to her parents and her sisters and a woman given to friendship. There was the close and lasting friendship with Geoffrey and Pamela Paul formed in their student days, her firm friendship with Philip Potter, one-time General Secretary of the WCC, and many others. With Brian Frost Pauline compiled the anthology *Celebrating Friendship*. It is fitting that her memoirs should be dedicated to Nadir Dinshaw, who shared Pauline's passion for 'justice only justice', and with whom she compiled the inter-faith anthology *Living By Grace*.

This book is a very good read, telling us much about Pauline Webb, and about the Church and the world in the twenty-first century. As I close the book I long for a companion volume of Pauline's collected sermons and talks; the sermons I remember from Sheffield and Vancouver, and others that she refers to, like the sermon at Philippi on the women who began the church there, and those three lectures on the ecumenical movement given in Vancouver as a visiting professor.

It is a great privilege to have been invited to write the Foreword for the book of a woman I so admire, who opened paths in the ecumenical movement that I have been able to tread. Through it all emerges a woman whose personal decision for Christ at an early age remains unshakeable, a woman who can hope against hope, even in the darkest situations. Her epilogue with its thoughts on ageing, being now 'in the departure lounge', will help those who seek to face growing old with equanimity and love.

Mary Tanner
June 2006

# 1

# *Join the Church and See the World*

❧

M y journeys to the ends of the world began at 1.45 pm on Friday 25 January 1946 in the chapel of King's College, London. There was only one other person in the chapel with me, a fellow student who had been trying to persuade me of the importance of making a whole-hearted, personal commitment to the Christian faith. Despite the gloomy, battle-scarred appearance of the chapel itself, I felt an awesome sense of the presence of God and an awareness of having reached a moment of crucial decision. I didn't realize then the full significance of that moment for me, nor was I aware that the day itself happened to be the feast day of the conversion of St Paul.

My experience in the chapel could only partially be described as a conversion. Like Paul, my namesake, I didn't suddenly turn from atheism to religious faith. The faith that blossomed into flower in that particular, personal encounter with Christ had grown from seed implanted many years before. I had grown up in a devout and loving Methodist manse and had never felt the need seriously to question the faith of my father and mother. As another child of the manse once put it, I had from infancy been so inoculated with religion as to be in danger of never catching the real thing! Yet eventually my two sisters and I each found our own particular way along different paths to a personal faith.

In my first term up at the University the confident faith and evangelistic zeal of some of my fellow students had almost bowled me over. Many of the freshers that year were six or seven years older than I was, for they had just been demobbed from the armed forces. They brought to their studies an impatience to get on with their interrupted careers and a serious outlook on life which came from having literally faced death themselves and dealt it out to others. For some, the grim reality of such experiences had shattered any religious faith they might once have had. For others, the support they had received from chaplains and from Christian friends and comrades in many parts of the world had led them to an enthusiasm for things spiritual and an earnest search for some signposts to a better future. Almost all cherished a determined dream of a time when war should be no more.

Those of us too young for active service had inevitably also felt the impact of the war upon our lives. Even when writing our papers for the matriculation exams on which our university entrance in those days depended, we had frequently had to dive under our desks in response to the droning of a doodlebug (flying bomb) just about to explode somewhere in the neighbourhood. I relished the irony of having to include in the middle of an essay on Caesar's Gallic Wars a note to explain that 'at this point we were interrupted for five minutes by enemy activity'. Yet we could not rely on any particular sympathy from the examiners. Knowledge of Latin was in those days still regarded as an essential qualification for those hoping to study for an Arts degree. 'In years to come,' our Latin teacher warned us, 'no-one is going to remember and make excuses for you because you were the war-time generation.'

Evidence that the war had only just ended was still plain to be seen all around us. In the Strand entrance to King's College there was a huge bomb crater (long since covered over to make a car park). College departments were trying to re-organize themselves after returning to their London base from long periods of evacuation. Fuel shortages were still so commonplace that we carried candles to our lectures in case the lights cut out and we kept our hands warm by cupping them round our cups of coffee.

Over those cups of coffee, like every generation of students before and since, we discussed what was wrong with the world and how we were going to put it right. Though the Student Union had none of the extensive facilities it enjoys today, it set before us at the 'Freshers' Squash' a bewildering variety of options, calling for our allegiance to this or that political party, suggesting diverse sports and leisure activities and, most pressing and persuasive of all, inviting us to various forms of religious commitment.

It was that word 'commitment' that scared me most. Surely, I felt, the time had come to explore all the different possibilities life might offer me, without committing myself to any of them. Politically, I had not yet decided which party I would belong to. My mother had been a Tory, my father a Liberal, but throughout the war we had known only a coalition Government, so there had been little party propaganda or political discussion at home. The election of the Labour leader Clement Attlee as the first post-war Prime Minister was as big a surprise to me as to many other people. Such great adulation had been given to Winston Churchill as the nation's undoubted leader in war-time that it was difficult to imagine the country being led by anyone else. Discussions with my ex-service fellow students, however, demonstrated to me that an interest in politics can encourage a long memory, and that past performance as well as future policy must be taken into account when electing a leader of government. I began to share the enthusiasm of those who dreamed of a new order of society and a welfare state enshrining the principles of socialism.

The possibilities on offer in the religious sector of the freshers' market were also many and varied. I was warmly welcomed into the comforting bosom of 'Meth. Soc.', the Methodist Society, but felt reluctant to accept a label indicating my particular identity at too early a date. King's, itself an Anglican foundation, had a strong theological faculty. This meant that the Student Christian Movement had a firm base and a formidable-looking programme of lectures by learned teachers of apologetics. I welcomed the opportunity the college gave to all of us to be introduced to theology in a series of lectures open to students of every faculty. In these lectures, intended to qualify us as non-theological Associates of King's College, the saintly Dean of King's at the time, Canon Eric Abbott, opened up to us the biblical basis of each of the phrases of the Apostles' Creed. I found it all fascinating but not at all decisive in helping me shape what I eventually wanted to do with my own life.

It seemed to me at the time that the possibilities of a career were severely limited, simply by the fact of my being a woman. I had long admired my father as both a preacher and a pastor and would have loved to follow in his footsteps. There had been a debate in the Methodist Conference shortly before the war, which almost reached the decision to accept women into the ministry, but because of the war no action had been taken. When eventually Conference got round to discussing it again, while I was still in college, the recommendation was rejected, to my total bewilderment and bitter disappointment.

When I turned to consider other possibilities, most paths seemed blocked to women. Though I was reading English, and loved writing as well as reading it, my head teacher had warned me against journalism, as I had not shown any particular interest in either fashion or food, the traditional subjects for women columnists. Fascinated as I was by the new art deco building in Portland Place, Broadcasting House, the headquarters of sound radio, I knew a little about the struggles of 'Women in Media' to persuade the BBC to employ more women news readers and correspondents. In those days it was still argued that to have women presenting or reporting the news would seem to trivialize its value and turn it into entertainment!

So it was that, equivocal about my political views, undecided about my future and unsure about my faith, I came into contact with the college's Christian Union. On being approached by Jeanne Brealey, one of their most enthusiastic and attractive members, who invited me to join their weekly meeting for prayer and Bible study, I made it clear that, interested as I was, I did not believe in being committed to any particular group at this stage. She refused to be deterred by my non-acceptance of her invitation, saying, 'There's only one decision that really matters. That's the decision to accept Christ as your personal Lord and Saviour. Once that is settled you will find that that shapes all the other decisions you will ever make.' She invited me to join her one lunch-time in what was then the still war-damaged and rather dingy college chapel. There, after some time wrestling in prayer together, I made the decision for Christ, or it felt more as though Christ made a decision for me. The words my friend had spoken proved true. Every other decision I have ever had to make since has followed on from that one. But I had no idea at the time how far it was all going to take me.

I was not the only person to be caught up in this new evangelistic zeal. On my first day in college I had found myself standing in the queue to register next to another student with the same initials as mine. As a result I fell into conversation with Pamela Watts, and, as we both later confessed to each other, we decided we might as well stay together until we got to know our way around and met more interesting people! However, the evangelistic enthusiasm of the members of the Christian Union proved infectious and only a week after my own experience of personal conversion, Pam experienced a similar religious awakening. Our friendship deepened into a shared, lifelong journey of faith. In college itself we eventually took over the leadership of the Christian Union. Geoffrey Paul, one of the ex-service men who had come to King's to further his studies in theology, became President of the CU, with Pam as his deputy and me as the secretary.

Our earliest attempts at public evangelism were almost disastrous. One of the popular apologists for the Christian faith at that time was the theologian and broadcaster C. S. Lewis. We boldly invited him to a meeting in the Great Hall at King's College and by dint of widespread publicity managed to attract an enormous audience, not only of the theological students, but of many more sceptical but curious unbelievers. To our horror and dismay, at the last moment, when the hall was packed to capacity with an eager, expectant audience, the great man failed to turn up! As we learned later, a sudden attack of 'flu had laid him low and there was no way he could contact us. So Geoffrey himself held the fort and also plunged me into my first experience of public speaking. As a result, even my eventual forays into Hyde Park with Lord Soper's open-air preaching teams never held the same kind of terror for me.

Geoffrey and Pam married, and went first to serve together in the Church of South India. Returning to England eventually with their five daughters, all talented in different spheres, they served the Church of England in many significant roles – in Bristol where Geoffrey was canon theologian, at Lee Abbey where he was warden, and then in Hull, where as bishop he gave a series of lectures on popular theology which was able to fill the town hall! Finally he became the greatly loved Bishop of Bradford. His untimely death robbed the Anglican Church of one of its most gifted, popular communicators of Christian faith to the secular world. The influence of that little group of enthusiasts in the Christian Union had thus spread across the world.

———

One of the slogans popular among Methodist youth leaders in my teenage years was the advice given to all members of the newly formed Methodist Association of Youth Clubs to 'live on a large map'. As the daughter of an itinerant Methodist minister, I had already experienced life in seven widely separated parts of the map of the UK, all in different social contexts. From the newly developing London suburb of Wembley, where I was born, we moved to the Midlands city of Leicester. Then on we went up north to the seaside resort of Morecambe, then the cotton town of Shaw, near Oldham and then the Staffordshire village of Audley, returning back to the London area during the war years. My father's earlier experience as a missionary in Western Nigeria gave him such a love of that country and of its people that we frequently had African visitors to stay with us. Their coming gave him the chance to practise his Yoruba, in which I am told he was fluent. I even learned some of the many words of greeting in that expressive language, and in other African languages, myself and these have stood me in good stead on many occasions since!

I first became most aware of the actual world map and the extent of the influence of the Church within it when I went to a youth conference organized by the Methodist Youth Department in 1948 under the title 'Anybody's World?' In the arrogance of my new-found evangelistic fervour, I had already made myself known to the people at the MYD Headquarters, mainly through critical comments I made on what I regarded as their 'unsound' theological emphasis on social issues rather than on personal conversion. Rather than entering into argument with me, to my surprise they invited me up to their offices to share in the planning of their conference, and even to act as one of the two vice-chairmen of it myself! They had invited as speakers some of the leading Methodist writers and theologians of the time. Their subjects ranged from Edward Rogers' talk on the challenge to Christian faith of the spread of communism, to Charles Davey's insistence on the need for a Christian code of personal morality in a world where conventional family values had been put under catastrophic pressure during the war years.

For me personally the biggest impact was made by the shy but substantially built and ecumenically renowned scholar, Ernest Bingle, who described the experience of having recently been in Amsterdam for the founding Assembly of the World Council of Churches. He drew for us a vivid picture of churches from many nations and denominations at last coming together after centuries of theological and ecclesiastical division, and after the recent tragic separation caused by two great world wars. He even drew a kind of diagram for us showing three different streams of Christian witness in the earlier years of the century: a concern for world mission, a concern for the unity of faith and order in the churches and a concern for active engagement in the life and work of society. Now, he explained. these three streams were to form this one World Council of Churches. He left ringing in our ears the confident, optimistic note of the Assembly's message to the churches, which ended with the determined slogan (originally penned by the wise and perceptive Anglican lay woman, Kathleen Bliss), 'We intend to stay together.'

A chance meeting not long afterwards impressed on me the idea that this ecumenical movement was not only, in Archbishop Temple's words, 'the great new fact of our era', but that it also offered new vision and hope to our up-and-coming post-war generation. An aunt of mine, eager to show hospitality to overseas students arriving in Britain, arranged a social to welcome those studying in London University and asked me to act as hostess. Among the guests was Philip Potter, the young Caribbean Methodist theologian who had been the leader of the youth delegation at the Amsterdam Assembly. I expressed to him my doubts about the 'soundness' of the theology underlying this new, ecumenical movement. Philip's own personal enthusiasm for all that had taken place at Amsterdam and the prospect it offered for the future of the world-wide Church was charismatic. What began then in our brief theological discussion blossomed into a personal friendship that has lasted for a lifetime. Philip has been one of the strongest influences moulding the pattern of my life and my view of the Church ever since.

The Church world picture was further brought to life for me in an unforgettable presentation at our own youth conference by missionary enthusiasts Muriel and Ernest Booth. This was long before the days of such technical sophistication as Powerpoint. They simply used a form of flannelgraph, whereby cut-out cardboard maps backed by scraps of wool adhered to a large blue cloth, making a simple but effective visual aid, which I remember celebrating in doggerel at the conference concert:

> The Methodist world picture was unrolled from east to west
> On Mrs B's blue blanket and Mr's hol-ey vest!

Having rolled up the world map as it were and put it in my case, I returned home to resume my search for some sense of vocation. It had been impressed upon us at the conference that if we ever hoped to be of any service overseas we needed to have a professional qualification. So it seemed to me that the obvious course to take was for a Teachers' Diploma at the Institute of Education. My tutor there was the Caribbean educationalist John Figueroa, an extraordinary figure – corpulent, bearded, jovial like a Falstaff, and gifted as both a poet and a broadcaster His deep voice with its soft Jamaican accent was well known to cricket fans across the world as one of the radio commentators for his beloved West Indian team. His edited collections of Caribbean poetry introduced me to a culture and a people which were later to become like home and family to me.

Living in Lambeth at the time when the MV *Empire Windrush* ship brought the first great wave of West Indian immigrants to Britain, my father tirelessly visited the homes of those whose names were given to him as having found accommodation somewhere in the locality. Many brought with them transfer notes from their home churches in the Caribbean, and expected to be welcomed by fellow Methodists in Britain as members of the same world-wide family. Shamefully, in some places their experience was one of rejection rather than of ready acceptance. To ensure that this should not be so locally, outside the church of which he was minister in Railton Road, Brixton, my father had a large notice board erected stating 'West Indians very welcome here!' Despite the disgruntled mutterings of some who feared the kind of change this might demand of the long-established white congregation, such a pro-active approach to the new arrivals had a positive effect on the life of the whole church. Today, like many other societies in the inner belt of London, Railton Road Methodist Church is a vibrant and thriving community, whose members are predominantly Caribbean in origin.

However, in my first teaching job, in Twickenham, we were living at that time in an insular, mono-cultural society. Thames Valley Grammar School was a suburban, co-ed. establishment. Its headmaster, H. W. Bligh, tried to make it as much like a traditional British public school as he could, encouraging a love of the classics by naming the school houses after classical heroes and composing a school song that celebrated the Latin motto, *Hanc Exorna!* (Bring honour to this place!) The school choir was enthusiastically trained by Lorna Brooks, a young music teacher with whom I immediately struck up a friendship that was to last a lifetime. It was such a happy school that my form (1P) has been holding regular reunions ever since. In those immediate post-war years we were aware that the world around us was changing rapidly and the youngsters were eager to take up the new opportunities for travel at last opening up before them.

My own first great desire was to travel to Germany. In the war years at school we had complained about having to learn a language regarded as the language of the enemy. A wise teacher, herself an exile from Germany, had assured us that one day we would welcome the opportunity to go to that country ourselves and turn our enemies into friends. So my first overseas visit was with a school exchange trip to a German Mission School at Hermannsburg, not far from the mediaeval town of Celle. Like any school excursion it was not without its toll of crises – lost passports, homesick children and occasional clashes of opinion between German staff and us, their English counterparts. The Germans took a much less relaxed view of school discipline than we did and they tried to inflict a somewhat regimented programme on our unwilling pupils! There were inevitably clashes of language too, such as when one young English boy was shocked to be asked politely by a German companion, 'Do you mind if I eat your flesh?' meaning the pieces of roast beef he had left on his plate.

The biggest shock came however one evening when, having been sight-seeing in Hamburg, we missed the last train back to Celle and began to hitch-hike home. Along came a lorry which took us as far as the village of Bergen, only about seven miles from Hermanns-burg. Then came the shock. We were right beside the Belsen concentration camp, now mercifully liberated, but still displaying its mass of graves of both former inmates and of soldiers slain in the recent battles. Our German colleagues protested that they had known nothing of the existence of the camp or of the horrendous crime against humanity committed there. But I found that hard to believe. The community in Hermannsburg was a pious,

11

God-fearing community and I wondered how it could ever be possible for a church to be so blind and deaf to what was happening in its own immediate neighbourhood.

The personal effect on me was that when the handsome young brother of one of my German colleagues (to whom I had secretly become attracted!) put his cloak round my shoulder in a courteous gesture, I suddenly realized it was a cloak that had belonged to a member of the SS. I threw it to the ground and ran from him in disgust. Clearly the wounds and even prejudices left by war were going to take a long time to heal.

Back at school I had taken on responsibility for Religious Education as well as teaching English. I became determined that in that curriculum we should include not only a study of biblical teaching, but also an emphasis on Church history and on the contemporary ecumenical movement, with all that it might imply for international relations in the future. I traced its beginnings back to the World Missionary Conference held in Edinburgh in 1910, out of which grew an International Missionary Council. There a multitude of different missionary societies from all parts of the world had come together to discuss a common strategy of mission. From the beginning of the century there had been what was known as a 'Comity of Mission' whereby different churches and denominations agreed to work in certain specified areas and not to trespass on to territory allocated to a different mission. This had already begun to make nonsense of many inherited ecclesiastical divisions. A fellow student from Uganda once told me how in his country, for example, Anglican missions had been successful in one area and Presbyterian missionaries in another. So the ludicrous situation had often arisen whereby a man who lived on one bank of a river would proudly call himself a member of the Church of England, whilst his brother living on the other bank of the same river maintained his allegiance to the Church of Scotland!

Within the classroom itself, I found that the children had little awareness of their own denominational history. I remember one girl asking me to explain the difference between the terms 'Protestant' and 'Anglican', and an earnest young Ms Malaprop asking me, 'If I become a member of the Methodist Church, does that mean that I will become a prostitute?'

The concept of 'foreign' missionary work grasped the imagination of the class. Some came with stories of 'real live' missionaries they had read about in Sunday School, as a result of which they cherished dreams of travelling to faraway places and performing great acts of courage and self-sacrifice. Albert Schweitzer and Mary Slessor were names they listed among their early-twentieth-century heroes and heroines. One girl enthusiastically invited the whole class to her own local church where they were holding a missionary exhibition. The visiting speaker on one particular afternoon was to be a world-renowned eye surgeon. No doubt welcoming the chance of an afternoon out of the classroom, I persuaded the headmaster to allow me to take with me any of the children who wanted to go, which inevitably included almost the whole class. We were rewarded with a fascinating and most moving account of the amazing results achieved in eye surgery in India, where literally hundreds of people daily were being treated for cataracts in a mobile surgery on a train that travelled the length and breadth of the sub-continent, giving, as the surgeon put it, sight to the blind. One of the schoolboys was so inspired that he decided there and then to be a surgeon himself when he grew up, and I confess to feeling some pangs of regret that I had not really seriously thought of offering to serve overseas myself.

Yet it was not the speech of the surgeon that made the deepest impression upon me. A remark made by the chairman of the meeting went on haunting my memory long after the meeting was over. He emphasized that the work we had heard described was made possible not simply through the skill and sacrifice of people like the medical staff. They depended greatly on the support of thousands of others who provided the financial resources and the spiritual back-up that continued to make the work possible. So he urged every member of the audience to resolve to do all they could to open the eyes of the blind, not literally in India, but equally important to awaken among the people of Britain a greater awareness of the needs of those living in other parts of the world. He suggested that every one of us should pray that we personally might be used to open at least one other person's eyes to a wider view of the world and of their role within it.

Now I have come to believe, through many years of experience, that prayer can be a dangerous activity! It sometimes seems as though God takes our prayers more seriously than we do. I hardly expected anything dramatic to happen in response to my personal prayer that I might be able to inspire a more global view in the children I taught. Yet then occurred one of those extraordinary coincidences which defy any rational explanation of how providential intervention can dictate the course of our lives. Only two days after I had attended that missionary exhibition, I received a letter from the headquarters of the Methodist Missionary Society, inviting me to go for an interview with those responsible at the time for their own Missionary Education Department. They were looking for some young person prepared to give two years service as a youth secretary, whose responsibility would be to make the 'Live on a Large Map' slogan a reality in the then rapidly growing Methodist Association of Youth Clubs. My name as a possible candidate had been suggested by that same Muriel and Ernest Booth, whom I had teased so mercilessly about their own attempts to unfurl a world map on a fluffy piece of flannelgraph!

My headmaster warned me against taking what he called a 'sideways step' at this early point in my career. Even other senior friends whom I consulted in the Church thought it sounded a risky, insubstantial offer. But at the time I heard a retired Methodist minister, who himself had a long record of distinguished missionary service, preaching a sermon about decision-making. He suggested that when you have to make a choice between two paths, one of which leads straightforwardly ahead whilst you cannot see where the other will lead, then faith may well require you to take the risk and trust God to work out his plan for your life. It sounded foolhardy advice but I decided to take it, though I confess that I hedged my acceptance of the post with all sorts of conditions about its only being for a two-year period. I even persuaded the headmaster to promise me my job back when I needed it – but as it happened I never had occasion to remind him of that!

My entry through the doors of the splendid headquarters of the Methodist Missionary Society in Marylebone Road proved to be the beginning of a whole new chapter in my life. Though I spent the first two years slogging it around the sometimes rough and rowdy youth clubs now mushrooming across London, I soon felt the need for training in methods of more effective communication. It was suggested that I took up lay preaching, which I had long resisted, partly because I was much aware of the prejudice still felt even in Methodist circles against women preachers. Instead I was encouraged to join Lord Soper's Order of Christian Witness, which required us to hone our skills in public speaking by taking to the open air and facing, as he did so skilfully, the onslaught of hecklers.

This was a period of great campaigns. Billy Graham, the American evangelist, was filling the Harringay Stadium daily. Many of the members of my own youth club in Brixton came with me to hear him and responded to the thrill of being part of these huge gatherings, with their spectacle and music and appeal for a definite decision for Christ. We followed up with regular meetings in the manse for Bible study and prayer, where even these so far unchurched youngsters began to develop their own liturgies. My habit of sitting on the floor when leading the meeting at home led to the ritual that whoever was the leader had to sit on the floor!

Meanwhile, in the field of missionary education, we realised that there too we needed spectacle and the inspiration of great occasions to inspire vision and commitment. We were coming to a time of great celebrations of missionary history – the bicentenary of the Methodist Church in the Caribbean, the centenary of Women's Work, and the beginnings of Medical Missions. For all these events we wrote and staged great pageants, each involving at least a thousand performers and all held in the inspiring ambience of the Royal Albert Hall which was filled to capacity on each occasion with an audience drawn from all parts of the country.

I came to realize that words written and dramatized could be as powerful as any words spoken. So, after my two years stint as a youth secretary came to an end, I was amazed but delighted to be offered the post of Editor for the Society. That involved producing a monthly illustrated magazine known by the imperial sounding title *The Kingdom Overseas*, and publishing books, pageants and plays that would help to enlarge people's awareness of the world-wide extent of the Church. When I was first offered the post I resisted on two grounds. I protested firstly that I was still too young for such responsibility and secondly that my own experience of the world overseas extended no further than to the Isle of Wight. My bosses replied that the first fault time would remedy, and the second fault they intended to remedy by sending me on my first major tour overseas. My assignment was to write a script for a film about the newly formed and united Church of South India. So my first world journey was about to begin!

———

# 2

# *Filming the World*

❧

My visit to India in the winter of 1956 was expected to take a couple of months. Then the world was plunged into political crisis. On the day we were due to sail on SS *Carthage*, the headlines of the day announced that on Colonel Nasser's orders the Suez Canal was to be closed to all shipping, except that which he permitted. This meant that our route would take us round the Cape of South Africa, landing us eventually in what was then known as Ceylon, and thence up into India by train. The outward voyage would take four and a half weeks. Ten weeks of travelling were planned in a variety of modes of transport for visiting the locations chosen for the film; and it was to take at least another four weeks to get home again! I phoned the Mission House to enquire whether in these circumstances it might not make better sense for me to switch to an airline. But in those days sea travel was regarded as being much better for the health and the process of acclimatization than the rapidly developing and still more expensive air travel. So, in the company of 14 missionaries, I set sail for the East under the leadership of one who was himself a sign of the new ecumenical times – the Rt Revd Frank Whittaker, a former Methodist minister, who had recently been commissioned as bishop in the newly formed Church of South India.

The long journey by sea afforded us plenty of time to learn more from the bishop and some of the senior missionaries about the vitality of this young, united church. It had been chosen as the subject of our film because it represented a church union of unique importance, though still at the time one which was causing considerable controversy, particularly in the Church of England. It had been inaugurated in 1947 after 30 years of negotiation between the united Presbyterians and Congregationalists, the Methodist districts and, most significantly, the Anglican dioceses in South India. The Anglican bishops, together with three presbyters from each of the uniting churches, had consecrated new bishops for the new church, drawn from the different traditions. They would henceforth have authority for the ordination of all new presbyters. Thus, the Church of South India conformed to the historic tradition of episcopal ordination, which has become a thorny issue in so many other union negotiations.

In the newly independent India this united church, enriched by incorporating within its life the best qualities of its constituent denominations, would be better able to reflect its own Asian history and culture. It had already recovered some of the lost traditions of the early church, which South Indian legend dates right back to the time of St Thomas. It had brought back into the liturgy of the world-wide Church the ancient tradition of the exchanging of a 'kiss of peace' among the congregation before the sharing of communion. The Church of South India was becoming, as our film title eventually expressed it, a *Bright Diadem* in the Indian crown.

Life on board what came to be known as our 'slow boat to China' (Hong Kong being its ultimate destination) soon took on a life of its own, with the fiercely competed games of deck tennis, the political arguments, the lavish banquets, the live entertainments, the shipboard romances and the visits ashore that characterize any long cruise. Thus, my own view of the world was already beginning to be challenged even en route to India.

Our first visit ashore was to Dakar on the west coast of Africa. It was my first glimpse of what we had come to call 'the third world'. The crowded market seemed unbearably hot and the goods on sale tawdry. I was horrified by my own reaction of revulsion from the first street beggars I had ever seen, displaying ugly human deformities. Back on board, the bishop had a serious pastoral job of reminding me what it means to share the compassion our Lord felt on seeing the needy multitude and he tried to prepare me for the shock of the poverty I would have to become used to in India.

Our next port of call had a different kind of shock in store. Our first view of the harbour at Cape Town was magnificent. It looked like a sunlit Mediterranean city set against an Alpine background. We were eager to explore its beauty. On board we had booked our seats for a coach tour which would include a journey up the mountain. Then we saw our coaches awaiting us on the quayside, lined up in two separate rows. Only then did we realize that we passengers were being divided into different groups according to our race.

It happened that I had brought with me to read on board the new book *Naught for Your Comfort*, written by Trevor Huddleston, the 'troublesome priest', who had recently been ordered home from South Africa by the religious community to which he belonged. Its angry impact came home fully to me in those first brief hours we spent in Cape Town. We refused to go on the tour and, in solidarity with Indian friends from the ship, staged our own pathetic protest on the quay, the first of many anti-apartheid gestures in which I was to become involved in later years.

Two weeks later we arrived at Colombo, which I saw at the time as a 'smiling' city. This was because I was met by an old school-friend, Margaret Pilling, who was working in the Colombo City Mission. She took me first on a shopping spree and then gave me a glimpse of the palm-fringed, luxurious beach at Mount Lavinia, promising me a couple of days' break there on the way back home.

Our journey was not yet over, and we had to take an all-night train ride to Talaimanar and then a boat across into India, entering by the back door as it were!

At a kind of comic opera Customs House, which was obviously not used to handling such large numbers of passengers, our passports were examined at least eight times. At last I was served on the train my first really hot Indian curry (I didn't know how to ask for a mild one) and settled down to another overnight journey, this time to Madras. I was struck by how the scenery changed to a much more luscious green and how all my senses seemed to be assailed at once by the bright colours, the loud noises, the pungent smells and the fabulous fabrics surrounding me everywhere in India.

Nothing had prepared me for the shock that awoke me during my second night on the train heading north to Dornakal. Suddenly, in my sleep I heard raucous shouting that seemed to be right outside my berth. I recognized the sound of my own name being called. I stumbled to the carriage door, where, still in my nightie, I was hauled out of the train and driven by two missionary colleagues to the bishop's home, where I was expected as a dinner guest. 'There was a time', his wife commented, 'when Europeans in India always dressed for dinner, but I don't remember anyone arriving in a night dress before!'

I learned after that always to expect the unexpected in India. My few days in the Dornakal diocese were packed with new experiences which provided more than enough material for the film script I had by now begun to write. My first most impressive visit was to a village where a retreat was being held for local women, who were mainly casual labourers in the fields, and who, like the majority of India's Christians, were from the community once known as 'outcaste' but then given by Mahatma Gandhi the title *harijan*, the children of God. Now as a result of their bitter experience of discrimination they are known as the *Dalits*, the oppressed.

To equip me properly for my visit I was taken to buy a sari and blouse and we packed a car with just what we needed for a weekend's camping – camp beds, blankets, toiletries, food supplies and some reading matter. It was only when we unpacked our luggage in front of our hosts in the village that I realized how everything we had brought as essentials for our needs must have seemed to them extraordinary luxuries! Nevertheless they welcomed us with garlands of flowers and invited us to enjoy the meal they had prepared for us. I learned how to sit cross legged on the floor and to scoop up the large helpings of rice and vegetables that were served to me on the banana leaves that acted as plates. I was embarrassed by the size of the portions I was given, especially when I realized that these women regarded themselves as fortunate if they had a meal just once a day – in times when crops failed and work was scarce they often ate only two or three times a week. Nevertheless, as my colleague explained to me, as long as I ate every grain of rice on the plate they would replenish it with yet another helping, thinking I had not yet had enough! Their own poverty was not allowed in any way to diminish their generosity to others.

During the retreat a communion service was celebrated, in which the local presbyter distributed to all of us small, equal portions of bread and sips of wine, saying in Telugu the familiar words of our Lord which came home to me with fresh meaning, 'This is my body, given for you – This is my blood, shed for you.' I realized perhaps for the first time the significance of the fact that these words were not just addressed to me personally but to all of us standing there together. A communion service can never be a solitary experience. It should always be an expression of community. We were all – we, privileged visitors from the West and those women, among the most oppressed of the East – of equal worth in the Lord's eyes. I decided there and then that the peak of our film should be the portrayal of just such a communion service, and that our theme must be the message of God's universal love which affirms the worth of every human being whatever their status, race or gender.

This was the motivation behind the extensive work of healing and teaching I was to see throughout the dioceses of both Dornakal and Medak. Central to it all was the worship of the church, enshrined in the Medak Diocese in a magnificent and anachronistic looking cathedral whose tower pointed up to heaven like that of an English parish church! But already in the Church of South India worship was changing in form, making more use of Indian lyrics and musical instruments. I visited places of retreat modelled on traditional Indian *ashrams* where disciples gather round a teacher who can give wise, spiritual guidance. Many of the educational projects I saw were based on Mahatma Gandhi's principles of Basic Training, developing the use of local products and native talents.

After a visit to the ancient city of Hyderabad I made my first ever plane journey, in a violent thunderstorm, back to Madras. Then in a slow, frequently stopping, overnight train I travelled on from Madras to Bangalore, my journey enlivened by the fierce political arguments that erupted in the carriage, sparked off by the news of the worsening crisis in the relations between Egypt and Britain. I was made nervous by the ferociousness of the anti-British feeling of my fellow-passengers, which was in sharp contrast to the graciousness I had experienced everywhere else in the country.

The main purpose of my visit to Bangalore was to see the United Theological College, where students were being trained together for the ministry of the Church of South India. It was from among those students that we chose our 'film star', Azariah, who came from Dornakal. We discovered later that he had originally wanted to be an actor, but his father had been a presbyter and had bequeathed to Azariah a box containing his own vestments in the hope that one day his son would continue his ministry. Now that dream was being fulfilled but, in another of those strange, possibly providential coincidences, it was just when Azariah had given up all thought of a film career that we arrived on the scene inviting him to star in our own documentary about the CSI!

In Bangalore I was introduced by the bishop to a retired deaconess, Sister Ethel Tomkinson, who was to be my companion on a journey through the Mysore Diocese and who impressed me as a saint beloved by the villagers and living as simply as they did.

The principal of the United Theological College at the time was the Revd Joshua Russell Chandran, the first Indian to be appointed to the post. He became one of the leading Asian theologians on the world ecumenical scene. Having been convener of the union negotiations committee that led to the founding of the Church of South India, he was able, through membership of the Faith and Order Commission of the World Council of Churches, to share the Indian experience with other churches engaged in union talks. It struck me that in those days so much of the impetus of the ecumenical movement was coming out of Asia through leaders of the calibre of Russell Chandran, M. M. Thomas and Daniel Niles of Sri Lanka.

It was decided that for the village sequences in the film we would travel yet further south, to the Tiruchirappalli Diocese. There we would be able to feature the work of Dr Anne Booth in a local Christian hospital and dispensary. There too we would be able to portray the all-pervading power and influence of Hinduism expressed in the city in the massive and photogenic Srirangam Temple, with its intricately carved columns, its throng of pilgrims and the riot of colour on its mass of market stalls. We visited too a new monastery built by the Ramakrishna revival movement, which has since become so well known to us here in Britain.

We journeyed out to the coast through magnificent scenery

where tall palmyra trees stood either side of the road like sentinels. Then ahead of us we saw the calm blue sea at Nagapattinam. The villages in the area were mainly Hindu but here and there we met isolated Christians who had asked for baptism. (Fifty years later I was deeply moved to hear on the Radio 4 programme *Turning the Tide* how that lovely coast had been ravaged by the tsunami of 2005, and how a Christian convert had turned the bitterness of his own grief at being bereaved of his own three children into the aid he now gives to hundreds of other children left homeless by the flood.)

It was in 'Trichy' that the camera team and director from Gateway films met up with me and I handed over to them my suggested story line for more detailed work on a shooting script. I stayed in the area long enough to be with them during the shooting of one sequence – a village communion service. I was deeply moved by the sincerity and the patience of villagers who had to stand many hours in the hot sun and who insisted only on the cameramen stopping for lunch, though they refused to take any food or any payment themselves.

My responsibility over, I journeyed yet further south to join my friends Geoffrey and Pamela Paul for Christmas in Trivandrum. Geoffrey, having become fluent in Malayalam, was teaching at the Kerala Theological Seminary training presbyters for the united Church of South India, and also coming to know and relate to members of the much more ancient Christian traditions in the area, such as the Orthodox Syrian Church and the Mar Thoma Syrian Church of Malabar. Pam, as well as looking after their growing family, was helping with work among the university students, introducing them to English literature, producing radio plays and reading modern poetry with them. We had a few happy days' break together enjoying the magnificent scenery in that part of the world, and being greatly entertained by Mandy, the eldest daughter, and

Lucy, my god-daughter, both of whom were at that stage charming toddlers.

Returning to Colombo, I saw the old year out literally with a bang as, during a Watchnight Service in the City Mission, whilst a memorable sermon was being preached by the Revd Denzil da Silva, we heard guns firing and fireworks exploding to announce the arrival of 1957. Tragically, later in the Ceylon that became Sri Lanka, guns were to be heard too often, not in celebration but in confrontation. Meanwhile, it was time for me to return home, albeit again by a roundabout route. But I wasn't complaining!

\* \* \*

The success of the film *Bright Diadem*, both in local churches and on national television, encouraged the Methodist Missionary Society to invest more time and resources in communicating its message through visual media. So a couple of years later, two more films were commissioned, both to be made in Africa, marking the coming of independence to Nigeria in October 1960. It was clear that, as Britain's Prime Minister, Harold Macmillan, was to say in that same year in his address to the South African Parliament, 'The wind of change is blowing through this continent, and whether we like it or not, this growth of national consciousness is a political fact.' It was a fact affecting not only the nations but the churches too. Churches which had been founded, governed and substantially supported by missionary societies in the West were aspiring towards an autonomy which would enable them to become a more integral part of their own national life and culture. Eventually, it was hoped, they might grow beyond the denominational divisions they had inherited from the West. As the Revd Egemba Igwe, who was to become the first Secretary of the Methodist Church in Nigeria, suggested, in a land whose new motto was to be 'Faith and Unity', the Church should make its aim 'One Church, one Gospel.'

It was decided that our first film should be a documentary of the work in the eastern area of Nigeria. We wanted to feature in it some of the new projects being undertaken by the church in education, medicine and evangelism. As two of the 'stars' we chose twins who, in an area where twin births had once been regarded with fear, could now look forward to a healthy, happy and fulfilled new life. For the second film we would concentrate on the work at the Uzuakoli Leprosy Settlement.

I was sent ahead to choose the locations and write the scripts for both films. Again I had to travel by sea, a journey that gave me twelve leisurely days on board and the chance of brief visits ashore, to Freetown, Sierra Leone and to Takoradi in Ghana, which whetted my appetite for return visits to both places many years later. Finally I arrived in Lagos, at that time still capital of Nigeria, a nation of 130 million people, made up of 250 different ethnic groups and covering an area of almost 370,000 square miles. I was thankful that my journeys were to be concentrated on just one small area of it!

From Lagos I flew directly to Port Harcourt. There were signs of new life everywhere. All around the oil refineries were extensive building sites and new roads being constructed. I was immediately made aware that Nigeria is one of the world's largest oil producers, an industry that has not only brought great wealth and extensive development to some sections of society, but has also fuelled dissension, violence and corruption in a country where there is an immense gulf between rich and poor and where the average life expectancy is still only 46 years.

The next day, by an amazingly intricate piece of organization of the kind which never failed to impress me when travelling over-seas, I was whisked up country in one car, met at a cross-roads by a car coming from another direction, and transferred with all my luggage to continue the journey through what must once have been dense bush country. Tall coconut palms and heavy banana trees flanked the road on both sides, so that it was like riding between high walls of green. In practically every village we passed through we saw signposts to the local Methodist primary school.

Then we met long processions of women coming home from the market, carrying their precious loads on their heads. One even had a new chair perched precariously above everything else, including a radio set! Eventually we arrived at our destination, Umuahia, the Methodist headquarters in the district, where I was allocated my own headquarters to work in for the next few days.

Before long I had been whisked off to the theological college, where I was asked to talk to the students and answer their questions about the Church of South India. Coming themselves from many different church traditions they were most concerned about the whole question of Church unity. Denominationalism, commented one student, was a legacy of the past that seemed totally irrelevant to the Church of the future in Africa.

Over the next few days I was invited to listen in on a series of district committees, which gave me an overview of the extensive and varied work the church was doing throughout eastern Nigeria and we planned visits to schools and hospitals, and many new churches in areas of rapid development. A long itinerary was planned for me, which included three days in the company of a lay missionary, Marjorie Weeks, and a team of local evangelists, trekking on foot, like old-time pioneers, through bush country in the northern area of Oturkpo. People we met there were hearing the Christian gospel for the first time. I had never realized before how effective the parables are in conveying the joy of the lost being found, the prodigal returning home, the sinner being forgiven, as these stories were enthusiastically re-enacted and people recognized the experiences they described.

My next visit was to the Uzuakoli Leprosy Settlement to work on the story we wanted to tell in the second film about the encouraging developments in the treatment of one of the most dreaded diseases in the world. I confess that it was with some trepidation that I arrived there, but I shall never forget the welcoming service I attended in the hospital chapel, where the gowned choir entered in procession led by their choirmaster and composer, Ikoli Harcourt Whyte, his own hands badly crippled by the effects of the disease many years earlier. They were singing lustily, 'Come, let us join our cheerful songs'. It was only as they passed by me that I could see that many were lame, some were blind and all had leprosy.

This was a place of real hope. Recent developments and research in the use of multi-drug therapy had made it possible for the disease of leprosy, if diagnosed early enough, to be alleviated. One of the great partners in the research into treatment with one of those drugs, dapsone, was my host at Uzuakoli, the Revd Dr Frank Davey who in the following New Year's list was awarded the CBE. Not only was he a skilled doctor and a beloved minister. He was also an enthusiastic gardener, which explained why the colony was surrounded by the most beautifully designed and picturesque gardens I was to see anywhere in Nigeria.

It was here too that I was to meet our 'film star', Priscilla, one of the permanent residents in the homes provided for the most disabled people. She had known all the stigma as well as the deformity associated with leprosy and had been rejected by her home village many years before. She told me, with a brilliant smile, 'No-one in the world has ever loved me as these people do'. It was her story that we decided to tell in the film, which we entitled *Beauty for Ashes*.

My preparatory work on the script over, I started the return journey home by flying back to Lagos and spending Christmas at Ilesha in western Nigeria, a place I had read and heard about since early childhood. My father had been stationed there as a missionary during the First World War. There he joined a lay colleague, and keen member of the Wesley Guild movement, Dr John Stephens, who had trained first as a pharmacist in Weston-super-Mare. Hearing of the great need in Africa, he had sold up his business, taken further training as a doctor and gone out to Nigeria to take charge of a dispensary in Ilesha where, with the support of the Wesley Guild, he founded a hospital which is still greatly respected, now under government control.

Dr David Cannon and his wife and children welcomed me to their home and took me out to see how the hospital had extended its influence throughout many surrounding villages in a research project seeking to counteract kwashiorkor, the terrible effect of infant malnutrition. In an area where 50 per cent of the babies were dying below the age of 5, it was a joy to share in the celebration of the fifth birthday of Bodunde, the first child to be enrolled in the project. She looked as healthy, happy and alert as any mother could wish. It was a great start to our Christmas celebrations. Then it was time for me to be back on board, steaming for home as we greeted the dawn of a new decade, 1960.

\* \* \*

Film-makers, like fishermen, tend to feel that their best catches are those that they never land. That was true of my third and last film assignment. It was scheduled to be made in Burma, whither I travelled (by air this time!) towards the end of 1962. In that very year General Ne Win had staged a military coup. For the second time within the past few years he had taken over government from U Nu, who had been the elected prime minister since the country became an independent republic in 1947, but who had been unable to quell the unrest of rebel forces and tribespeople living in the hills.

It was a fiercely cold winter, and we were held up by fog for 24 hours before leaving Gatwick. Once we were airborne, the views from the clear blue sky were spectacular. Flying over north India we could see below us dry, brown plains with villages splattered over them like the blots shaken from a mud-clogged pen. Then the pilot pointed out to us in the distance over 100 miles away the peak of Mt Everest. Soon below us we could see the teeming city of Calcutta and the twisting creeks at the mouth of the Ganges, until we crossed the Bay of Bengal into Burma, where in glittering sunshine we landed in Rangoon.

Even in the customs hall I began to feel uneasy. It was clear that the army were now fully in command. The fact that I was listed as a journalist aroused suspicion. When asked the name of the journal I represented I replied confidently *The Kingdom Overseas* and was alarmed at the officer's immediate reaction. 'Whose kingdom do you mean?' he asked, accusingly. 'Burma is now an independent state and we have turned our back on British imperialism.' I attempted an elementary theological definition of the title. Apparently mystified, he waved me on.

I was met by the Revd Stanley Vincent of the Bible Society who took me to Bible House in the centre of Rangoon, a busy, modern city with neon-lit advertisements making it look like an oriental Piccadilly Circus. There were several cinemas, one showing, surprisingly, *Ben Hur* and the others more salacious films. To complete and enhance the scene were the floodlit, fairy-like pagodas. The great Shwe Dagon pagoda was familiar to me from photographs but it was more beautiful than I had imagined, with its golden spire tapering gracefully above wooded fields and streams where saffron-robed Buddhist monks strolled at leisure.

Stanley took me with him to friends for my first taste of Burmese hospitality. We banqueted at a circular table, with an inner section that kept circulating, placing in front of us an exotic selection of eastern dishes. The company and the conversation at the table were gracious. I was particularly struck by the confident dignity of the women guests, many of whom, it seemed, had kept their own names after marriage. In some cases they were in jobs of higher status than their husbands and kept control of the family finances. When I expressed surprise at this state of affairs, one woman explained that there was a tradition that Burma was once a matriarchal society and that women on the whole enjoyed equal status with men and played an active role in political and economic life. Yet I later discovered that women were still unrepresented in most traditional male offices and barred from some professions. I could see for myself, for example, that Buddhist nuns are given nothing like the same respect as the monks, who are the most honoured group in Burmese society.

The small Christian community in Burma has many distinguished women leaders. Among them was Daw Mi Mi whom I had met the year before in England, where she was representing the Church in Burma at a special Overseas Consultation held to discuss the future role and relationship of the churches in newly independent nations. Having been educated at the Wesley Girls' High School in Mandalay and trained as a teacher in Rangoon, Daw Mi Mi had escaped to the jungle during the years of the Japanese occupation. On her return home she immediately opened new schools, at first holding classes in the open air. She took on increasing leadership in church work and became the first circuit steward in the Mandalay circuit. She had recently married U Ba Aye, Chairman of the Burma Christian Council Christian Homes Committee.

Having met her and other women leaders like her in Burma, I

was not surprised in years to come to learn of the continuing courageous stance of the Nobel Peace Prize winner and pro-democracy leader, Aung San Suu Kyi, in opposing the increasingly repressive military government of Burma (now known as Myanmar). Despite world-wide protests, she has been under frequent sentences of house arrest over the past 18 years.

It had been decided that for the film in Burma we should focus on three areas, all at different stages of growth and development. The total Christian community throughout Burma is small, numbering in all just under a million in a total population of about 50 million people. We were eager to see how local leadership was being developed and how the church itself was moving towards total autonomy.

The headquarters of the Methodist work was in Mandalay, Burma's second largest city and also the heart-centre of Buddhism, which in 1961 had been declared the official state religion. We arrived in Mandalay on the day of a great festival when crowds were flocking to the Arakan pagoda, the most famous among the mass of pagodas on the hills dominating the city. The atmosphere among the pilgrims was so jovial as to be almost Chaucerian. The pagodas were surrounded by colonnades of shops like colourful bazaars and we watched a hilarious concert being performed in the precincts. It was different from the quiet meditation I had always associated with Buddhism. That I was later to experience when I was privileged to be given an audience with an elderly, spiritually serene abbot who had founded a Buddhist monastery where young monks were being trained in the disciplined and meditative study of ancient sacred scriptures.

The church, in its work among the Burmese, put a lot of emphasis on the distribution of Christian literature, and on the use of films and drama as ways of telling the Christian story. Accompanied by the superintendent of the Burmese Methodist area, the Revd U Hla Thaung and his wife, I travelled out to the nearby towns of Monywa and Kyaukse, where the Revd Ted Bishop and his wife Barbara, missionaries from Britain, were still stationed. I was impressed by the work of Burmese colporteurs enthusiastically selling Gospels in the market. One of them, U Bo Tun, had once been a *pongyi* (boy monk) himself when he had read a copy of St John's Gospel and was particularly gripped by the concept of the Logos 'by whom all things were made'. Now he was so eager to sell the Gospel to others that in the half hour I was with him, he sold 21 copies of the New Testament!

In contrast to the small size of the Christian community in Mandalay itself, there were some impressive Christian institutions such as the Theological Institute, the schools, the Leprosy Home and the Bailey hostel which provided shelter for some of Burma's poorest street children. We were clearly going to find plenty of material for our film within the Burmese area alone.

More exotic adventures lay ahead. Within a few days of arriving in Burma, accompanied by a veteran missionary, Florence Cleaver, we travelled up from Mandalay to Kalewa in the Chin hills, there to board a boat chugging up the river Chindwin as far as Homalin. We were joined by an Irish family, the Turtles – the Revd David, a Methodist minister, his wife Maureen, a doctor, and their three small children of whom Simon the youngest was just two weeks old. They were travelling back to the Somra Tract, where work had been established only within the past 12 years among the Khongsai people, who, driven by famine, had migrated into Burma down from the Naga hills.

The river journey up to Homalin took five days, so we were fortunate to travel in a well-appointed vessel which had once belonged to the President of Burma. It was a slow journey up-stream, turning and twisting to avoid sand-banks and stopping every night at some riverside village, where we usually went ashore for a brief visit to a local store or café. During the day the river was full of traffic, with sampans and canoes and water buffaloes to keep us watching on deck. At Homalin we disembarked and had to wait some time to hire a small motor-boat into which we somehow managed to cram not only the seven of us but all our luggage and Maureen's medicines and equipment as well.

The welcome awaiting us from the crowds gathered on the river-bank was ecstatic. The Turtles were greatly loved in the village, where Maureen, who was the only doctor around for over a hundred miles, had a throng of grateful and of still needy patients. She and David, who assisted her, were renowned for her ability to treat people suffering from trachoma, saving them from blindness through simple surgery or protecting their eyes with the application of aureomycin ointment.

The village of Maingdaungphai was built on the edge of the jungle, with homes centred on a football pitch and a church already established there. While Maureen stayed behind to set up her clinic, David took me and Hope Musgrave, the woman worker, to visit some more recent settlements. As we pushed our way through the dense undergrowth along muddy paths between trees where apes really did swing to and fro, I was reminded of the war films we had seen of the fighting in the jungles of Burma. But we received a most peaceful welcome and tried to share with the Khongsais the promise of peace on earth which we were celebrating in what would be for them their first Christmas.

We were invited to stay overnight in one of the houses built up on stilts, where we were able to lay out our sleeping bags on the wooden floor-boards. I don't know what was the bigger shock to me during the night – to hear neighbours snoring beside me, or the pigs under the house snorting beneath me!

During the night, Hope, who was not a medical worker, was called to an emergency in one of the houses nearby where a young girl was having a miscarriage. With only the contents of a first aid box available, Hope did what she could to help the girl amid all the smoke and grime of the surroundings, and stayed with her while we went back to the village to ask Maureen what more could be done. When I told Maureen how helpless we had felt not knowing what to do, she replied, 'It is worse, knowing what needs to be done but not having the resources to do it.'

The next day was Christmas Day and in Maingdaungphai we were awakened at 4 am by carol singers who led us into the church, festooned with coloured lanterns and balloons, and nativity scenes recycled from old Christmas cards. The people came crowding in wrapped in thick blankets, looking like Bethlehem's shepherds as they each went forward to put gifts in a huge basket at the front of the church – a box of matches, a handful of rice or a small coin. The preacher was a young man whose eloquence I could recognize even though I couldn't speak a word of his language.

After the service followed the feast – venison from the deer brought in from the jungle on a pole the day before and jacket potatoes, apparently a favourite delicacy among the Khongsais. Then came the entertainment – a hilarious concert, for the young people were talented mimics and had their own brand of pop music sung to skiffle instruments.

I was sad when the time came to leave Maingdaungphai but confidently began imagining what a wonderful sequence we would be able to film there, making full use of so much inborn but undiscovered talent.

My next destination was down river again, at Tahan, at the foot of the Chin hills where there was a flourishing church community among the Lushai people, who had brought their Christian faith down with them into Burma. They were different in temperament from the Khongsais, and seemed to have inherited an evangelistic enthusiasm from the Welsh Calvinist Methodists who had worked among them in the hill country many years before. Certainly, one could detect a strong Welsh influence in the hymns they sang, sometimes to melancholy settings of traditional Lushai lyrics, and sometimes to the strong harmonies of Welsh tunes sung in a minor key. This hymn-singing seemed to be their major form of entertainment. It would often continue all through the night at what was called a *leng khawm*, a gathering of a large crowd in one of the long houses, and would have an almost hypnotic effect on those who stayed throughout the whole session.

During the day there were lively services in the local, newly built chapel where people prayed fervently, not only one at a time, but lifting their voices together to express whatever was most on their minds and hearts. Whilst I was there, staying with the Revd Claude Nurse and family, the news from Britain was of fierce blizzards and bitter weather, and it was heart-warming to hear those Lushai women praying earnestly for their 'cold, cold sisters in Britain'.

The young people in the church community who belonged to what they called the YCA, the Young Christian Association, were eager to help with the film. Many of them were aspiring young actors and actually presented me with a suggested script! I decided to take up their ideas in a series of photographs which we could make into a film-strip even if we never got around to making the film. This proved in the end to be a premonition.

The director and cameramen were planning to come to Burma within the next few weeks, but by the time I got back to Mandalay, hoping to send off the draft script, bad news was awaiting me. The military government had announced that all foreign missionaries would soon be compelled to leave Burma. It became certain that the film-makers would never be given visas. More seriously it was clear that the tribespeople, with whom I had spent such a memorable time, and the whole Christian community in Burma would suffer under much harsher restrictions in the near future.

---

So I came back with just film-strips and memories to inspire us to keep the people of Burma in our prayers and in our concern through all the troubled years that lay ahead.

The church in Britain has kept up contact with the church in Burma as much as possible ever since, through occasional visits to and from the Burmese area, through frequent correspondence, through regular prayer and through participation in the many protests that have been made against the abuse of human rights. Since the time I was there the church has grown and there are now more than 16,678 members of what is known now as the Methodist Church in Upper Myanmar, which includes the Tahan District. There are still active associations for both women and young people. The church is a member church of the WCC. How I regret that I could bring back no permanent record on film of what had been for me a memorable visit to the hospitable, hopeful and richly diverse peoples of this fascinating land.

## 3

# *Wanting to Change the World*

᠁

I came back from my travels to what seemed a complacent post-war Britain. People were beginning to believe Prime Minister Macmillan's superficial assurance (whether he meant it seriously or not) that they had 'never had it so good'. But a new mood had erupted in the theatre. A seminal play by a young playwright, John Osborne, had opened at the Royal Court Theatre in 1956. *Look Back in Anger* flew in the face of contemporary theatrical convention. Its setting was far from romantic – a small, dreary attic flat. Its leading character was the anti-hero Jimmy Porter, who looked out in disgruntled cynicism on a world where there seemed to be no longer any great causes worth fighting for.

> 'Oh heavens, how I long for a little ordinary human enthusiasm!' he exclaimed, 'just enthusiasm – that's all. I want to hear a warm, thrilling voice, crying "Hallelujah, hallelujah, I'm alive!" '

Osborne was the first of many new playwrights who were dubbed 'the angry young men' and their plays became known as 'kitchen sink drama'. Arnold Wesker's *Chicken Soup with Barley*, first performed in 1958, traced the effect on a Jewish family of the past two decades, beginning with the activism of the anti-fascist demonstrations in the East End of London in 1936 and ending with the disillusionment of the Hungarian uprising and suppression in 1956. The play ended with a plaintively optimistic plea to the leading character, Ronnie, who says he doesn't care about anything any more. In the last words of the play he is told, 'Ronnie, if you don't care, you'll die!'

In this era of 'angry young men' it was a shock to me personally when the popular press decided to label me 'the angry young woman'! This was their reaction following a speech I made at the Methodist Conference of 1957. I was still reeling from the shock of the impact on me of my first close glimpse of third-world poverty. The theme of my short intervention in a conference debate about overseas missions was the need for the Church to issue a much tougher challenge to the young people of my generation. Though we looked back in anger on childhood memories of war we wanted to look forward in hope to a different kind of world. Sometimes it seemed as though we had nothing to fight for and nothing to fight against. Calling young people to follow Christ, I pleaded, must mean much more than inviting them to belong to a church youth club, or to embrace a personal faith that made no wider demands upon them. They must be summoned to care more passionately about people in other parts of the world and to engage in a world-wide battle against hunger, poverty and disease. Some might be encouraged to go overseas themselves to give voluntary service. (Voluntary Service Overseas was just about to begin at that time.) Others should be urged to take part in well-informed campaigning for a better world order.

Up to that point in the conference, it had been a fairly lethargic debate on a warm summer's day and the press had taken little notice of the proceedings. My sudden outburst, as an unexpectedly youthful participant, seemed to wake the journalists up. The next day, the *Daily Mail*'s headline declared, 'An Angry Young Woman Startles the Parsons'. All the other papers followed suit. The *Guardian* headlined my phrase about young people being 'fed up with a too kind state', whilst the *Yorkshire Evening Post* featured me patronizingly as 'That Girl in Blue'. It must have been a slack week for news, because the story then ran for over a week, being taken up by the Dean of St Paul's in a special article in the *Daily Telegraph*, and it was made the subject of a topical radio sketch by the popular comediennes Elsie and Doris Walters. Most embarrassing of all for me, the *Daily Sketch* sent a young 'cub' reporter (David English, later to become Editor of the *Daily Mail*) to stalk me for a week and publish a series of articles ostensibly in my name, analysing the state of modern youth and the need for radical changes in the Church's work among them!

Like many people who are subject to media attention, I wanted to escape from it all. I crept into the conference the next day, feeling that I had made a fool of myself. I shall ever be grateful for the comforting, encouraging words of Dr Donald Soper (later Lord Soper), who himself so often experienced the kind of unexpected exposure one's speeches can excite in the media. 'Never mind,' he said, 'they may have made a fool of you, but it's worth being a fool for Christ's sake!'

One unexpected outcome of this notoriety and of my film-making expeditions was that they gave me an entry into what was then the rapidly developing medium of television and especially the experiments being made in new ways of meeting the requirement for religious programmes. The film we had made in Nigeria called *Beauty for Ashes* was featured on the ABC's regular Sunday evening youth programme known as *Sunday Break*. It's interesting to note that the film provoked a letter to the *TV Times* protesting against such a sad and upsetting story being shown in a programme aimed at young people!

Penry Jones, who was ABC's Director of Religion, was eager to discover and train more clergy to communicate in this demanding medium of television. The churches had already begun their own small training centre, under the inspired leadership of the Revd

Cyril Thomas. He persuaded me to join in auditions Penry was holding, as a result of which I was enrolled on a week's training course at the Didsbury studios of ABC Television. A great deal of publicity was given at the time to the fact that I was the only woman and the only lay person to be included in a course for potential religious broadcasters.

It was the custom then on commercial television that programmes ended every day with a three-minute religious epilogue, usually broadcast from a studio no bigger than a broom cupboard, with a fixed camera gazing at the presenter through a large glass eye. I remember being told that the art of broadcasting was to speak as though one were addressing a single viewer, like one's grandmother sitting comfortably at home. I protested that my grandmother didn't have a glass eye, and that in any case, at that late hour of night it would seem more appropriate to address one's remarks to a younger viewing audience!

On the course we tried our hand at a variety of programmes, including a kind of docu-drama on the life of St Paul and an attempt at presenting in contemporary newsreel form the account of the slaughter of the innocents. Both programmes eventually made it on to the air and, after further training in script writing, I was given several more assignments including a life story of John Wesley which we entitled *Man on Fire* and a programme on the controversial topic of women in the Church, which was presented by the popular broadcaster Ludovic Kennedy.

Meanwhile in my own job at the Missionary Society I had an extensive and exhausting programme of what we called in those days 'missionary deputation'. We were expected to visit local churches in many different parts of the country, addressing large public meetings as well as preaching at two services every Sunday. There was a massive job of education to be done, helping people to move from old concepts of overseas missions as a kind of spiritual imperialism emanating from the West, into an understanding of the growth of autonomous churches in independent lands from whom we in the West had much to learn. The films we made, the magazine and books we published and the many large events we organized were all tools with which we tried to make people more aware of the world-wide nature of the Church and of the changing form of the Church's mission within it.

During the next few years I thus had many platforms from which to communicate the concerns that had so fired me with anger. There were four main themes that dominated my speaking, writing and broadcasting. First was the continually haunting memory of the poverty I had seen among street beggars in the towns of Africa, in famine-stricken villages in India and among the neglected tribespeople of upper Burma. Here in Britain immediately after the war the churches had co-operated in responding to the needs of refugees caught in the aftermath of war through an organization known as Christian Reconciliation in Europe. That co-operation continued as the focus shifted to the clamant needs of the developing post-colonial world. Under the inspired leadership of the indomitable Janet Lacey that organization had become an integral part of the British Council of Churches and changed its name to Christian Aid. It became one of many mushrooming agencies bringing to light the facts about world hunger, trying to alleviate its effects and campaigning against its extent. I became an ardent supporter, street collector and advocate on its behalf.

To me this campaign seemed an evident outworking of the gospel of Christ who came particularly to 'bring good news to the poor' and identified himself with the hungry in their need. The concern was by no means exclusively a Christian one. The campaign against world hunger gained momentum among many young people. I remember attending one Sunday morning a meeting held in the Roundhouse, the former engine shed at Camden Town. It was clear that most of the audience were not churchgoers (this was after all a Sunday morning), but the main speaker was the radical Roman Catholic priest, Helder Camara, who had become archbishop of the city of Recife just at the time when the military had taken control in Brazil. Known as the friend of the poor he had become a controversial figure, and despite his diminutive stature was a charismatic speaker and a towering prophet in the growing concern about world hunger. I remember his saying to this large, mainly jeans-clad audience, 'I don't know whether you would call yourselves Christians or not, but if you are standing alongside the poor, then in my estimation you are standing right alongside Jesus Christ'. To my surprise the remark won great applause from what I had conceived to be a totally secular audience.

The second issue on which I had been stirred to anger during my few hours in South Africa en route to India had been apartheid and the racism that motivated it. This was contrary to everything I had been brought up to believe about the one human family created by God and to all the enrichment I had already known in my own life through the friendship of people of other races and cultures. Soon after I arrived home from Nigeria, I heard that Father Trevor Huddleston, author of *Naught for Your Comfort,* was addressing a rally in Trafalgar Square, along with Hugh Gaitskell and Jeremy Thorpe, to launch a campaign to boycott trade with South Africa. A few weeks later came news of the massacre in Sharpeville, in the Transvaal, in which 69 Africans were shot. So when, in the summer of 1960, the Anti-Apartheid movement was officially inaugurated, resolving to work for the total abolition of apartheid, I became a member of it and was present at many of the movement's subsequent protests in Trafalgar Square.

There was also increasing racial tension in Britain. In 1958 race riots in Notting Hill hit the headlines, sparked off to some extent by appalling housing conditions and exploitative rents. The church responded promptly. Lord Soper, who was then minister at the Kingsway Mission, recruited three of the most gifted and visionary young ministers to form a team ministry based on Notting Hill Methodist Church, charged with the mission of building there a vibrant, multi-racial community.

It was at about this time that I was 'laid aside', as it is sometimes expressed, by an illness which kept me in hospital for about six weeks. Actually I was laid on my back with a slipped disc, for which in those days total rest was prescribed. It gave me time to take stock of my life. I had reached that age when, like Bridget Jones, I was beginning to fear being left 'on the shelf'. During my illness, the care and concern shown to me by a former college friend of whom I had become fond led to his making me an attractive proposal of marriage. I had always thought that to be happily married must be the best state in life for any woman, but to be unhappily married must be a far worse state than being single, happily or unhappily. A friend whose own marriage had proved unhappy warned me, dramatically. 'It would be better to stay on the shelf than fall off it and break your heart!'

The problem I faced was that in those days it was generally accepted among Christians that a woman who married would make her priority the care of the home and any children there might be and give up all thought of a career. Clearly I was not deeply in love or I would have been prepared to give up everything else. I had fallen in love earlier in my life, but then the object of my affections was already married, so that relationship was never allowed to develop. Now, my old fear of making a personal commitment when I wasn't totally sure of what I wanted made me hesitate. Much as I would have loved a family of my own, I felt so fulfilled by the work I was engaged in that I opted for the single life.

---

Fortunately, close friends have since become a family for me, and other people have been generous in sharing with me the enjoyment of being with their children, to many of whom I have had the satisfying, but not too demanding role of being godmother or 'auntie'.

Maybe it is not surprising therefore that a third great concern in my life became the role of women, and the opportunity given them to fulfil their vocation whatever that might be. I had seen how, even in a society like Burma, with a matriarchal tradition, women were prescribed to play certain roles and prohibited from filling others, while in the official religion of the country they were afforded only inferior status. In Nigeria I had met women who had economic power in the market but a subordinate place in the home. In India I knew many highly gifted women of distinction and dignity but I was still aware that daughters were regarded as of less value than sons. In all the countries I visited the plight of poorer women concerned me most. It was on them that the burden of poverty fell heaviest and it was they who were the most vulnerable victims of oppression, violence and exploitation.

It seemed to me that, despite the model set by Jesus as one who honoured women and gave serious attention to what they had to say, the Church in general still relegated them to a second division. I had seen women missionaries sometimes working alone in difficult situations, and I greatly admired their dedication, skill and resourcefulness. Yet always, even in the Church, they worked under male leadership without the same kind of remuneration or recognition as the men.

I had been fortunate thus far in the responsibility I had been entrusted with and the male colleagueship I enjoyed, but I had on occasions experienced the kind of prejudice most women preachers were still subject to in those days. Though even John Wesley had to admit that some women seemed to have exceptional gifts, until the beginning of the twentieth century his followers forbade women to preach. Methodism still refused to accept the ordination of women to the ministry of word and sacrament. Although I had at one time wondered whether I had a call to the ministry I had therefore set that aside and sought a vocation elsewhere.

I felt it was time that the decision of the church was challenged once again. So in the Conference of 1959, following a report on ordination I begged leave to open the whole issue of women's ordination once more. Various procedural difficulties were raised to prevent this happening but eventually a commission was appointed to consider the admission of women to the ministry and to report back to the Conference. There followed another seven years of deliberation and debate.

Some of the arguments used against the ordination of women seemed to me extraordinary, often based not on theology, psychology or any other kind of logic but merely on prejudice. When I said this in the Conference I was given the rejoinder that it was all a matter of biology! This ribald remark provoked great laughter. But the interesting experience was that, as the years went by, the debate developed into more serious considerations. There was careful biblical study of the context in which Jesus lived and in which Paul wrote, and close attention to what was happening in other Christian traditions. In the Anglican communion during the war years in Hong Kong the Revd Florence Lei-Tim-Oi had been ordained priest to meet the pastoral needs of congregations separated from the mainland. In Sweden Dr Margit Sahlin became the first Lutheran woman priest in 1960. She told me of the kind of ridicule she had been subjected to at the time from those who opposed her ordination. One had even accused her of being 'another wound in the Body of Christ'.

The movement for women's ordination was gaining momentum throughout world Methodism too. In the USA, the Methodist

General Conference in Minneapolis had given full clergy rights to women in 1956; in New Zealand, Phyllis Guthardt was the first woman to be ordained a Methodist minister, in 1960. In British Methodism, when the opponents began to focus on minutiae such as what women would wear, what they would be called and whether they would be prepared to go out on pastoral calls late at night, the laughter changed sides in the debate and I sensed that we were winning the argument. The only objection to our immediately going ahead with women's ordination that I had any sympathy with was the ecumenical argument that this would seriously delay the developments towards actual Church union. These were beginning to reach an advanced stage in the relations between the Church of England and the Methodist Church.

The fourth major concern in life that I cared deeply about was Church unity. I had become a frequent advocate at meetings across the country commending the latest report on the Anglican–Methodist Conversations. I have always resented the fact that women are unjustly made to appear such a major threat to Church unity, as though male orders had hitherto all been ecumenically recognized as valid! It was the hope of those of us arguing for women's ordination that this would eventually be seen as a gift acceptable to the whole, united Church, and that all orders of ministry would be open to women as well as men.

Although I had long given up any thought of ordination for myself and had found a different form of lay ministry, I was eager to take further the rudimentary theological study I had done at King's College. My attempts at trying to communicate matters of faith within the discipline of three-minute popular, broadcast scripts had made me aware of how inadequate and even at times incomprehensible so much of the traditional language of religion had become beyond the circle of the pulpit. Theology, or 'God-talk' as John Macquarrie called it, needed to be re-interpreted. It was not just a matter of simplification. Even words of only one syllable – 'God', 'sin', 'death', 'love' – express such profound thought that they need to be re-minted in terms of contemporary experience. What, for instance, did the Beatles mean by 'All you need is love'?

It was at this time, when I was struggling with attempts at finding a new language of faith, that there burst on the world a paperback on theology that caused a sensation. *Honest to God*, written by John Robinson, Bishop of Woolwich, and published by the SCM Press in 1963, created a greater stir in the secular press than any religious book had done for decades. The bishop had already achieved notoriety by defending Penguin Books for their decision to publish an unexpurgated version of D. H. Lawrence's novel, *Lady Chatterley's Lover*. Now his critics claimed, in the words of a leading article in the *Church Times,* that he was 'apparently denying almost every Christian doctrine of the Church in which he holds office'. In fact he was doing nothing of the kind – he was trying to set Christian faith in the framework of modern, scientific understanding and to express it in the language and imagery that could be understood by people living in contemporary, increasingly secular society.

It was not so much the argument of the book that intrigued me. I admired the attempts to find new ways of describing God as being present in the depth of the human search for meaning rather than high up somewhere in a fanciful heaven but I became particularly fascinated by the book's footnotes and the references to so many modern theologians whom I had not yet come across – Dietrich Bonhoeffer, Rudolf Bultmann, Paul Tillich, Alec Vidler, to name but a few. I longed to have time to catch up on all this stimulating reading rather than ploughing on as I had been doing with a correspondence course on theology which seemed to take me little further than the Church Fathers!

*Honest to God* became the talking-point of many a lunch-time conversation at the headquarters of the Methodist Missionary Society. Among my colleagues there by this time was Philip Potter, the first minister from the overseas church to have become an Area Secretary. His responsibility extended over the Caribbean and the Americas and permitted him to give time to the World Student Christian Federation. With him was Harry Morton who had for a time worked in the scholarships office of the World Council of Churches. When I shared with them my personal ambition to have time off to do serious theological study, they put their heads together and came up with the idea that I should apply for a scholarship to the Union Theological Seminary in New York, whose list of former staff included such eminent names as those of Bonhoeffer, Tillich and the Niebuhrs. They encouraged me also to apply for assistance from the Fulbright Foundation which enabled British students to travel to the United States and vice versa. So, having persuaded the Methodist Missionary Society to agree reluctantly to my having a year's sabbatical leave, I was all set to go to New York in the September of 1964.

Then at the Methodist Conference of that same year I had a shock. I was nominated and immediately designated as Vice-President of the Conference (the leading lay office in the Methodist Church) for the following year. It was totally unexpected as I was the youngest person ever to be thus elected, and it was still rare for a woman to hold that office. I felt almost petrified by the thought of becoming part of the establishment at a time when the whole established order in the Church seemed to be called in question and when there was such a theological ferment brewing!

Meanwhile, however, the Union Theological Seminary in New York had awarded me a scholarship enabling me to share in what was called a Program of Advanced Religious Studies. This special course was laid on for a group of fifteen of us, all from different countries and from different denominational traditions. It was to be an experiment in ecumenical community, as we lived together in the same block of apartments and were encouraged to experience many different forms of church life both throughout the city and further afield. The Fulbright Foundation provided the cost of the fare, and so my next great adventure abroad began with my five-day journey, sailing for New York on the *Queen Mary*.

# 4

# *Letters from America*

*(Extracts from letters home)*

*10 September 1964*
*On board RMS* Queen Mary *(Cunard Line)*

We had a great send-off from Southampton. It was a memorable sight watching this giant ship setting sail. People ashore in the Ocean Terminal building were standing and waving to their friends. One group had a huge banner with the teasing slogan '*Go home, Yanks!*' Last-minute messages were called out and all visitors hurried off the ship. Then a huge crane pulled up the gangway and the band began playing, 'Now is the hour for me to say Goodbye', which we thought a bit grim! We set sail in the streaming sunlight, still waving to the colourful crowd fading into the distance.

*13 September*

We arrived at Cherbourg at about 7 pm and by the time we set sail again I was sound asleep as we could feel no movement at all. The steward woke me with a cup of tea next morning at 9 am by my watch, as on each subsequent day the clocks were put back one hour to accustom us gently to the change of time zone. I've spent the time getting to know many other Fulbright scholars on board. So far the ship has kept strictly to schedule. There was an announcement that we would pass the *Queen Elizabeth* at 2.40 pm and at precisely 2.40 we did.

*15 September*

After a stormy night we entered New York harbour and the giants of the Manhattan skyline emerged out of the mist, a sight so familiar from postcards that it seemed unreal. We watched the ship dock and excitedly prepared to disembark. Then the tedious waiting began. Having just seen the Statue of Liberty welcoming us to this new world, we were firmly locked into the Smoking Room to await the arrival of the Immigration Officer. Two hours later, we were able to come off the boat and out through the chaos of the Customs shed. Eventually I got away and looked for a taxi to take me to the address I had been given. We were told this was a Jewish holiday, so few taxis were available. After some hard bargaining I found a driver to take me up town, beyond the city's traffic jams, along the tree-lined river bank and up into our destination, Claremont Avenue, a quiet street across the road from the Union Theological Seminary. . . .

I found my home on the top floor of the block of flats allocated to our ecumenical, international group. I am sharing a flat with the other two women in the group – Gwyn Griffith, a cheerfully enthusiastic YWCA officer from the United Church of Canada, and Kirsti Kena, an earnest scholar from the Lutheran Church of Finland. There are twelve men in the group, all of different nationalities and from different denominations. Two of them are Roman Catholic priests, one from Goa and one from French Canada. They were introduced to us by our Director as 'gifts from Pope John XXIII', because, as he put it, 'Before Vatican II they would not have come and we would not have invited them!' I've already met also a Presbyterian from Ghana, the bishop of an independent church in Kenya, a presbyter from the Church of South India and a Methodist minister from Korea, all members of our group. There should be some interesting debate ahead!

*20 September*

I think one of the biggest surprises about coming to college in America is that superficially it seems like home as all the notices are in English. Yet their content is often quite unexpected. I was astounded today to read a note from the principal assuring students that if any of them were to be arrested during Civil Rights demonstrations, they could apply for help from what seems to be a college bail fund! Clearly it is expected that theological students will become politically active, inspired by the 'dream of freedom' so eloquently expressed by the Baptist preacher Martin Luther King in the huge rally at the Lincoln Memorial in Washington last year.

We are given a wide choice of courses in which to enrol. The whole group meets every week for lectures given by major leaders in the world-wide ecumenical movement, such as Kenneth Scott Latourette, Eugene Blake and John Bennett, Principal of Union. In addition to that I have opted to go to classes in Systematic Theology, Practical Theology, Old Testament, St John's Gospel, Mission Studies and Religion in Drama and Literature.

*27 September*

I'm finding the Practical Theology an interesting course and already have a paper to write on 'The Theology of the Laity', for which I intend to draw heavily on the book Dr Eastwood gave me on *The Priesthood of All Believers*. Systematic theology, I'm afraid, I shall find heavier going. Dr John Macquarrie, the renowned Scots theologian and author of *Twentieth Century Religious Thought* (pub. SCM 1963), has been inviting us to examine all the traditional arguments for the existence of God, leading us to the conclusion that most of them need to be jettisoned! Presumably he will bring us through the wrecks of 'natural theology' to find somewhere 'the Ground of our Being'.

*9 October*

We have spent the weekend at a group retreat in a place called Yorktown Heights. It's been sheer heaven to get away from New York into a rural setting. We stayed in a lovely old farmhouse, where the grounds were full of maple and birch trees, whose leaves were such bright crimson and gold that it looked as though the woods were on fire. We welcomed the chance of both physical and spiritual recreation, reading *Life Together* by Dietrich Bonhoeffer, who was for a short time a teacher at Union Theological Seminary until he left New York to return to Germany and confront the rising Nazi menace, at the cost of his own life.

We played volleyball, went for long walks and had a hilarious concert, for which I wrote a skit about our various idiosyncrasies, and said of our two RC priests, for example:

Emilien and Eliseo are very far from home
We expected unanimity along the path to Rome.
But now they've started arguing, how can we know what's true
When even the one Catholic Church is sometimes split in two?

We are such an unusually mixed group that we attract a lot of attention. Yesterday when I was out for a walk with our big, beloved African bishop, a police car drove up and asked me whether I needed help! I was sitting on the grass, and the bishop was standing over me brandishing a large cane. I had to explain that all was well – we were merely discussing episcopacy and Matthew was demonstrating to me the ceremony in which he himself had been consecrated.

*16 October*

Last night I had a party at my flat, finishing up the last spoonfuls of the real tea I brought from home (I don't like these American tea bags!). I'd invited all the British students I know here so that we could listen on my short-wave radio to the British election results. It looks as though Harold Wilson has a tough time ahead, with such a small majority!

*23 October*

Everyone here is as mystified by our method of electing a Government as we are by theirs. Frenzy is mounting now as election day approaches here too. Being at such a progressive place as Union, I haven't met anyone who thinks Goldwater even has a chance. Here students are wearing buttons declaring 'Goldwater for President in 1864!' . . .

The British election didn't get much of a press here but the *Sunday Times* gave a good review of the new cabinet and also the news of racial tensions in Britain. I think Americans take a kind of comfort in this, as they are so guilt ridden now themselves on this issue. The passing of the Civil Rights bill has been an attempt to mould the mores by legal enactment but it remains to be seen how successful that will be.

*25 October*

Most Sundays now I go across town to East Harlem, to join in worship at the Protestant parish there. This is the church that is so vividly described in Bruce Kenrick's book *Come Out the Wilderness*. The team ministry he wrote about in that book became the inspiration for the group ministry that has been set up at Notting Hill. To get to East Harlem we had to make our way through some really grim slums, as poor as the streets we'd seen in Naples. We arrived there on the day of the parish's 16th anniversary, so there was a big service of celebration.

This was informal, with everyone sharing concerns and calling for prayers of intercession. The sermon was a gathering together of thoughts contributed by people who had taken part in a Bible study during the previous week, and contained many references to personal experiences both at work and in the home. For communion an ordinary loaf of bread was brought in, and broken into hunks to be shared out among the people. Then a chalice of wine was passed round, and people began singing spontaneously and most reverently some of the haunting tunes of the spirituals.

*4 November*

We were invited yesterday to the home of our Ethics professor, Dr Roger Shinn, to join a group watching the results of the presidential election. We shared the general delight at the outcome, giving Lyndon Johnson a strong majority, but it was a bit shattering to realize that over 20 million Americans had voted for the reactionary Goldwater!

*8 November*

I'm writing this from Plainfield, a suburb of New Jersey where I've been preaching this weekend in a 'Negro Episcopal Church', at the invitation of their Jamaican priest who had been a fellow passenger on the *Queen Mary*. You should have seen the glorious procession as we walked into the crowded church – the choir in sparkling white surplices, the acolytes in scarlet cassocks, retired priests and the present priest in richly embroidered liturgical vestments, and me at the back in my rather dull brown London University hood and gown. We followed the full Anglican Order of Morning Prayer and I was asked to preach on Church unity with the theme, 'The Church as the Body of Christ'. Then in the evening I was unexpectedly whisked off to the major church in the town where there was a host of Anglican clergy gathered from all over the area, wanting to question me about the Anglican–Methodist conversations in Britain and our theological understanding of episcopacy.

*3 December*

I've got a 'Take home exam' this week on Systematic Theology, so I'm wrestling with questions like 'Compare Barth and Tillich in their conception of the relationship between reason and revelation'. I've been battling with Barth's *Doctrine of the Word of God*. Although I find much of the language he uses difficult, I find Barth's emphasis on the importance of preaching a great challenge. I appreciate even more the sermons of Paul Tillich, published under the title *The Shaking of the Foundations*. Most of them were preached originally in the chapel here at Union, where I still see him occasionally walking the corridors. It surprises me now that anyone ever thought the Bishop of Woolwich particularly revolutionary. What he was saying in *Honest to God* about the need to find new language in which to express theology was being said by so many of these great preachers and theologians over the last half century.

## 9 December

I was privileged to be invited by the Nigerian ambassador to the United Nations, whom I had met at a party, to go to see a debate there during a meeting of the General Assembly. The bishop and I were driven in a diplomatic car to the imposing UN headquarters on the east side of Manhattan. Just as we entered, Kenneth Kaunda was making a speech on the inauguration of Zambia into the UN. It was moving to join the whole Assembly in a standing ovation to this great African statesman at what was one of the crowning moments of his career. I found the UN a most inspiring place of hope in a world which seems once again to be trembling on the brink of crisis.

## 21 December

You will by now have received my card written in the plane on the way down to the Bahamas where my friend Mary Hocken and I have come to spend Christmas, at the invitation of Anne and Philip Blackburn. Philip, who always claims he has 'a mission to the rich', had arranged for me to speak immediately on my arrival in Nassau to a group of wealthy and influential laymen, on the theme of 'The Place of the Laity in the Church'.

The next morning I was whisked off to fly to the island of Grand Bahama 50 miles east of Nassau to see the amazingly rapid development taking place. Where six years ago there was just a mangrove swamp there is now Freeport, a growing town of 7,000 people and many developing businesses. This has all sprung from the dream of one man who saw the possibility of utilizing the resources of the natural harbour and turning the island into a bunkering place for ships where they could be refuelled at a far cheaper rate than anywhere else. A Development Corporation has sought to provide all the 'amenities of modern civilization', to quote the publicity, which means luxury hotels, casinos and super stores, with a school, a medical centre and a couple of churches thrown in for good measure! The school, which has begun under Methodist auspices, already has over 500 pupils, and is in desperate need of staff. The Church is facing enormous opportunity there if only it can find the resources.

## 29 December

We spent a boisterous Christmas day with the Blackburn family and their two small children. The highlight of the celebration was on Boxing Day when we were wakened at 5 am by the traditional carnival, known in the Bahamas as the *junkanoo*. The colourful costumes were ingeniously made out of rags and strips of paper and depicted all kinds of historical scenes. The procession, accompanied by twelve bands (all playing different tunes), took three hours to pass along the main street.

Then we moved over town to stay with Edwin and Madge Taylor. Edwin, a Barbadian, is the minister of Wesley Church, which has a black congregation as distinct from Trinity, Philip's church, still predominantly white. The Bahamas seem tragically to be the most racially segregated of the Caribbean islands. We heard rumours of sex discrimination as well. Philip told me that Trinity had said they would not want a woman to preach in their pulpit (though he persuaded them in the end reluctantly to invite me to do so). Wesley on the other hand welcomed me as their preacher with real West Indian warmth!

*31 December*

Just a postcard from Jamaica! We really feel as though we are on holiday now. We were thoroughly spoilt in the Bahamas but we were glad to get away from the tensions between the races and in the church. We were invited to come here by Hugh Sherlock, who is almost a legendary figure in Kingston, having founded a thriving Boys' Club, which has produced some of the West Indies' famed cricket team! He is universally known as 'Father' Sherlock.

After meeting us at the airport Hugh took us for a drive across the island to the north coast through magnificent, luscious mountainous scenery, a welcome contrast to the flatness of Nassau. We were taken to the Tower Island hotel for lunch, and enjoyed an afternoon of sunbathing, swimming and lazing on the verandah. Tonight I shall be preaching at a watchnight service at Providence Church. Then we go back to New York to face more lectures, term papers and exams! I wish we could take the sunshine with us and send some to you too. A happy 1965 to you – it's going to be a busy year for me!

*7 January 1965*

The flight back home to New York was the most magnificent I've ever made. We looked down on the deep, deep blue waters of the Caribbean sea, and its scattered green and gold islands. We could see Cuba clearly, with its still under-developed land. Then we landed in Nassau and met Edwin briefly again. On we went travelling down to New York through the sunset. Across the sky it seemed as though there was a great, elongated rainbow right across the horizon, dropping down into the sea. Suddenly there was a sparkling octopus of light, with huge fingers pointing up into the sky. This was Manhattan, and we were home, back to a freezing temperature, the clattering subway and milk shakes at a local drug store. Then – back to work! I've six papers to write and two exams, all in the next two weeks.

## 10 January

As I write this, the radio is playing solemn music, interspersed with hourly bulletins about Winston Churchill's health. It's unusual to have so much British news here in the States. It seems just like the grand manner of his whole life that he's clinging on so tenaciously at the end and keeping the world waiting until he's decided it's time to go! I guess the trumpets will surely sound for him on the other side!

## 26 January

Term starts tomorrow and we've been choosing our courses. I shall be going to a seminar on New Patterns of Mission, an ethics course on Christianity and politics, studying Reinhold Niebuhr's writings and a course on the Church in Urban Society, based on Harvey Cox's new book *The Secular City* and on Colin Wilson's *Where in the World?* Our Old Testament class focuses on major biblical motifs and is taught by James Muilenburg, who looks and speaks like an Old Testament prophet himself. To complete the package I've chosen a practical class on Religious Broadcasting. . . .

I have an interesting weekend ahead. I've been invited to visit friends in North Carolina, for several speaking engagements at the Methodist church there. This will involve a 14-hour journey by Greyhound bus, but it means I will get to see a different part of the country.

*1 February*

Here I am, way down in Dixieland. We had a fascinating journey through deep snow, coming via Washington. This was the first time I've seen the capital, which impressed me as much more elegant and dignified than New York. Our next stop was Richmond, Virginia. The countryside had changed to tall pine forests and gentle rolling hills looking particularly lovely in the freshly fallen snow. I had to change buses, with a long wait, at Winston Salem, a charming place that still has an atmosphere of peace, no doubt reflecting its origins as a Moravian settlement in the 1760s. I arrived in the dark at Mount Airey to a warm welcome.

Rachel Holcomb, my hostess, recounted to me with rapturous enthusiasm all the details of Winston Churchill's funeral which she had watched on television and I, unfortunately, had missed. 'You British sure are good at funerals', she told me, and contrasted it with the funeral of President Kennedy a couple of months ago, which she felt had been much less well planned. I pointed out to her that the circumstances of the funerals of these two great states-men were quite different – the one long prepared, the other, tragi-cally, totally unexpected. . . .

On Sunday I preached at the broadcast morning service, which I still find quite a nerve-wracking experience. But here in the States people are always appreciative of sermons though they usually congratulate me on my English accent, rather than on what I've actually said. One girl told her mother she loved listening to me because I sounded just like the Beatles! I felt I couldn't have had much higher praise!

*3 February*

Mount Airey is a small town with an old-world Southern charm. On Monday a couple from the church took me into the Blue Ridge mountains over into Virginia. On the rough mountain side we saw some mean dwelling places, homes of the Appallachian 'poor whites', one of the poorest groups, I was told, in the States. In contrast I visited the home of one of the church members, which was like a small palace. One thing I've noticed about wealthy Americans, whose homes have every kind of gadget you've ever heard of, is that they tend to take up handicrafts too, so you see in their home a loom for weaving or a pottery kiln or something like that.

*7 February*

When I got home from North Carolina I found my flat-mate Gwyn getting up every morning at 6 to go across to East Harlem to help during the school boycott there. The schools in this area are nothing like as well-equipped or staffed as the white schools, so the local people are protesting about this. The East Harlem Protestant Parish is sharing fully in the protest, so I agreed to go and help at the 'Freedom School' that had been set up there. It's hard work, doing mathematics (or 'math.' as they call it here) and social studies with a bunch of rowdy teenagers, but some seem keen to learn. I was asking them for the names of capital cities in the world. They suggested that the capital of the USA was Alabama, and the capital of England was Liverpool.

*10 February*

This week the news has been dominated by the crisis in Vietnam, which has provoked keen political argument in our group. I think our discussions reflect the influence Reinhold Niebuhr has been having upon us. Before his retirement he was a professor of Practical Theology here at Union, and his books are prescribed reading. They have certainly awakened in me a greater awareness of the relation of Christian faith to the reality of modern politics and diplomacy, and the need for a more stringent analysis of the 'just war' doctrine.

*8 March*

I left New York early last Friday morning to catch the 6.50 plane to Ohio, where I had been invited to preach at a Women's World Day of Prayer service. On the flight I had the indescribable experience of seeing dawn come up over the sea, lighting up the Manhattan skyscrapers in fiery red. It was a good beginning for this world day of prayer, which led me inevitably to think of the hymn associated with this day:

> As o'er each continent and island the dawn leads on another day
> The voice of prayer is never silent nor dies the strain of praise
>     away.

To my astonishment when we arrived in Ohio there was a thick blanket of snow. The service was preceded by a special luncheon attended by various dignitaries, all of whom were introduced to everyone else in speeches stressing how important everyone was! The service was broadcast and limited strictly to one hour, so I was warned to keep my eye on the red light while I was preaching and not to go one second over time, which was difficult as the rest of the service was extremely long! . . .

---

On Sunday I was on the air again, preaching at the morning service in an ornate church with a great deal of ritual and ceremony. Lights kept coming on and then dimming again at various appropriate points in the service. I noticed in the pulpit a list of code signs to give to the lighting engineer – like 'hand down cheek means lower house lights', 'finger pointing to eyes means spotlight preacher', 'hand up cheek means bring up gallery lights'. I had an almost irresistible impulse to make all the gestures simultaneously and see what happened! The whole service then had to be repeated for a second congregation, again numbering over 700 people. . . .

I've just received a letter from the Revd Ephraim Alphonse, a Jamaican missionary and a hero of mine from childhood days, inviting me to Panama for Holy Week.

*15 March*

This week has been tense at college. Several of our students had been down in Selma, Alabama last weekend, joining Martin Luther King's demonstration demanding voting rights for all citizens whatever their colour. There was a great contingent of clergy there supporting him. Then came the news that a gang of thugs had murdered one of the Unitarian ministers. There's a sense of shock throughout the college. It was infinitely moving at college prayers to hear all the students singing 'Faith of our Fathers – we will be true to Thee to death' and to know that most of them meant that quite literally.

*18 April*

It's Easter Sunday and here I am in Panama City. During this past week I have crossed the American continent 8 times in all and preached in eight different services. (I ought to explain that the isthmus here is only about 50 miles across.) I arrived just over a week ago on an overnight flight via Miami. Within an hour of my arriving Ephraim Alphonse had already got me involved in the case of a woman who had been taken off to gaol for having the wrong identity papers. He took me with him to visit her in the gloomy prison but fortunately he was able to sort things out for her and she was released. . . .

My first preaching appointment was in a new church in Rio Abajo, a suburb of Panama. Then Onafre, Ephraim's son, drove me to get the train to Colon on the north west coast. The people here are descendants of the West Indian immigrants who made up a large part of the labour force that built the Panama Canal, but who were evicted from the canal zone once the building work was finished. They settled, jobless and homeless, in what was then the ramshackle town of Colon. Over the years it has grown into the second largest city of the Republic of Panama and become a free port where many international firms have their South American supply depots. Much of the labour is casual, so many people in Colon are caught up in a vicious circle of unemployment and poverty. Seven years ago, Vic Watson was here as a missionary and founded a school with a scholarship fund to cater for under-privileged children, which now accommodates 250 children. Peter Swinglehurst is the current President of this Escuela Metodista. . . .

The next day I had to leave on the 3.30 am plane to Bocas del Toro, an island off the north coast where I was welcomed by Alan Francom, a probationer minister living here with his young wife and two small children. Their manse is built out into the sea, and even has its own pier where Alan's canoe is moored. He has pastoral charge of fifteen churches scattered throughout many small islands. I was taken for an excursion to an island about an hour's canoe journey away, called Coco Cay. Church work started there among the local Valiente Indian people only five years ago under the initiative of a young teacher, Santiago Smith, who had once worked in the mission with Ephraim Alphonse. The people have now built their own bamboo chapel where they were all waiting patiently to meet me. They were sitting on tree trunks, men on one side, women on the other, and the babies in the middle, swinging in net hammocks suspended from the rafters! At first we couldn't see any other children until the teacher pointed up to a precarious looking platform built across the rafters, where a giggly, shy group were waiting to sing some Indian songs for us!

It was terribly hot and I was relieved when one of the boys shinned up a tree, cut down a coconut, chopped off the top of it and gave me the coconut milk to drink. That must be surely one of the most refreshing drinks in the world! . . .

The next morning we had to travel by train, out through the banana plantations to catch a plane due at 9 am. The distance was only 23 miles, but we actually arrived at the air-strip at 10.15 am, the train having stopped every few minutes when the driver got off to help load bananas, which to him were more important than passengers! By way of compensation the pilot offered Alan a free flight back to Bocas del Toro. I flew on to Panama City. . . .

On Good Friday I was able to take part in a traditional Methodist Love Feast, which included a long and intense period of testimony. Then I got away again to Colon, where the Swinglehurst family took me for a beach picnic and swim. In the evening we watched a most colourful and poignant Good Friday procession through the streets of the city before I had to fly back to Panama. . . .

Easter Sunday services began early in the morning with a service for workers in the Canal Zone, followed by a service in the main Methodist Church in the city. This was fully liturgical, complete with the canticles and Prayer Book responses which have remained traditional throughout West Indian Methodism. Ephraim led the service and I preached, and he insisted on my sharing with him in the distribution of the Communion. Tonight I have to leave at 2 am to catch the plane back to New York after this memorable Easter week

### 29 April

I went yesterday to a posh lunch at the Statler Hilton held by the United Church Women. For the first time Roman Catholic women were invited as well as all the other denominations. So there were a few nuns in their habits mingling among the flowery hats and fur stoles of the American Protestants. One of the main speakers was Sister Mary Luke who was one of the few women invited to attend the sessions of the Vatican Council. She was a witty speaker. She told us, 'The Vatican Council is at last speaking to women, but as yet women are not allowed to speak to the Vatican Council.' One of the best parts of the programme was that we had three solos from Mrs Martin Luther King who is a professional singer and a beautiful woman, totally supportive of her husband's campaign for Civil Rights.

### 5 May

Ever since I got back from Panama I've been busy catching up on writing term papers and preparing the speech I'll have to deliver at Conference when I get home.

However, life has not been without its lighter moments. Sunday was a glorious day, the first real day of summer, which seems to arrive suddenly here. Gwyn and I decided to visit one of the off-beat churches we had heard about in our 'Local Congregation in Mission' lectures. It was the Judson Memorial Baptist Church in Washington Square, in Greenwich village, a kind of Soho-cum-Chelsea area of New York. We had heard that this church was experimenting in new ways of worship.

---

The service was due to start at 11, but when we arrived we found people standing round in groups chatting, or gathered round the piano singing favourite songs. The atmosphere was rather like that of a cocktail party. Then we were all invited to sit down. The minister chatted to us for a little while about 'liturgy and life', which led to a lively discussion about how worship could become more like celebration. Dishes of food were brought in – the kind that is served at a party buffet, with a bottle of chianti and another of grape juice. After a brief grace the minister read the words of the institution of the Lord's Supper and we shared the food around, drank the wine and juice together (according to taste). Then we shared news with one another and spent some time thinking about people whom we specially wanted to remember. Someone mentioned an area of particular need overseas and a plate was passed round for gifts, which were received with thanks. We were all given a blessing and that was the end. It was only afterwards that we realized that there had been all the usual ingredients of worship but in a totally informal setting. I wonder if that's the shape of things to come in the church, or will worship remain traditional?

*10 May*

We have had our final dinner together as a group and are now saying our farewells and beginning to shop and pack, ready for the journey home. It seems to me that in our small group we have embodied the diversity of the ecumenical movement but we have discovered the possibility of its unity too, especially as we have shared meals and prayers and new thinking together.

*19 May*

I feel as though I've started my journey home today. Gwyn has invited me to stay with her and a group of friends in Canada for a few relaxing days. I'm taking no pens nor paper nor books. I intend to be completely idle!

*25 May*

When I arrived back at Kennedy airport at 11.30 last night it hit me that I'm now really on my way back home. I arrived back to an empty room, my trunks having already gone to the boat. I've had a wonderfully lazy time in Canada. After two days looking around Toronto and visiting the fantastic Niagara Falls we journeyed 100 miles by road up to Gwyn's log cabin beside a magnificent lake. We were joined by friends celebrating a national holiday marking Commonwealth day. It was lovely lying out on the rocks in the sunshine listening to the lapping of lake water and dozing off to sleep. The only interruption was when we went for a short car trip and I fed a bear with a bottle of Coca-Cola! . . .

Tomorrow one of the students is coming to take us by car to the pier. There are six of us travelling on the boat together so we should have good fun on board. We arrive in Southampton early on 1 June and I reckon we'll be back home by lunch time. I don't mind what you give me to eat so long as it isn't fried chicken – I've had enough of that here to last for the rest of my life. For dessert I'm dying to taste good custard again! So there's your order.

Thank you for all your letters. This will be my last letter from America.

# 5

# *A World Parish*

❧❧❦

'Are we yet alive?' With this extraordinary question the Methodist Conference, the representative body of the community of Methodists in Britain, begins its annual session. It's the first line of one of Charles Wesley's rousing hymns. It's not only traditional, it's also appropriate. The Conference is a kind of annual check up on the health of all aspects of the Church's life and prescribes the policies designed to ensure its growth and development in the future. Already, seven years before I was due to take up office as Vice-President, the prophetic Dr Donald Soper (later Lord Soper) had famously commented at the Conference of 1958, according to the *Methodist Recorder,* 'It would be very hard for a casual visitor in this Conference to deny that he is in the presence of a dying Church – I do not believe that there is any permanence in the Methodist Church as a separate institution.'

His remark was immediately countered by statistics that indicated that there were two new Methodist churches being opened every week. Although Methodism, along with all other denominations, was beginning to experience the increasing secularization of society and a post-war drift away from regular church attendance, there were vigorous experiments going on in new areas, and bombed buildings were being replaced by modern suites of premises. At the time of the Conference of 1965, Methodist membership figures in Britain stood at almost three-quarters of a million. This nevertheless marked a decrease of about 10,000 on the previous year, a measure of decline that has gone on ever since.

Lord Soper's argument, however, had not been about numbers, but about the irrelevance of denominationalism in modern society. He saw the need for Methodism to make its own distinctive contribution within the life of the one holy, catholic (in the sense of 'world-wide') Church which he believed was being called urgently in the twentieth century into unity of witness and mission. Relations between the Church of England and the Methodist Church were becoming much closer, out of economic necessity as well as from ecumenical commitment. Where new towns were being built, it no longer made sense for different denominations to lay separate claim to land and resources. Local ecumenical projects were developing across the country, where premises were shared and team ministries were being formed.

In addressing the great political and social issues of the time, it was important for the churches to speak with one voice. The British Council of Churches, inaugurated in 1942, was by that time well-established as the main voice of the Anglican and Protestant churches acting and speaking together. In the growing crisis in Southern Rhodesia, where Ian Smith was threatening to declare unilateral independence, the BCC had issued a statement urging the British Government to delay the granting of independence 'until the representation of all citizens irrespective of race is accepted as the aim of Southern Rhodesian policy, and until there is in fact at least equal representation of Africans and Europeans in the Parliament of Southern Rhodesia'.[1] This statement was supported by all the main church leaders and endorsed by the Archbishop of Canterbury.

---

1 Resolution adopted by BCC 23 April 1965.

On this and many other issues there was increasing dialogue between the Anglican and Protestant Churches with the Roman Catholic community, which was itself undergoing great change as the result of Vatican II. Ecumenical optimism was so confident that Church leaders were even speaking of the possibility of celebrating one united Church in England by Easter Sunday 1980!

For me, coming hot-footed from the rich experience of living, breathing and studying ecumenism throughout my year at Union Theological Seminary, it was an opportunity of sharing that enthusiasm with the wider audience of the whole Methodist community. The President and Vice-President of the Conference are expected not only to make major addresses at the beginning of the Conference itself but also to speak on numberless occasions throughout the year in an exhausting itinerary that takes them to every part of what Methodists call affectionately 'the Connexion'. I was invited to preside over the opening of many of those new churches that were being built, to speak at numerous school speech days and to join in a great range of special functions, at all of which for that one year my colleague, the President, the Revd W. Walker Lee, and I were treated as celebrities!

It happened that 1965 was a year of celebration for two organizations in which I had a special interest. It was the twenty-first birthday of what had become the highly successful Methodist Association of Youth Clubs, the largest voluntary youth organization in the country at the time. I, once a member of an MAYC club, was one of the guests of honour at the special reception and dinner held at the Cumberland Hotel to mark the occasion. I had the privilege of meeting there for a second time the main guest of honour Princess Margaret, who was accompanied by her husband Earl Snowdon. Both of them showed a lively interest in the kind of activities youth clubs were able to provide for young people. The princess had shown similar interest in the outreach of the Church when I had met her earlier in the year at the opening of a new Methodist International House at Penarth.

Another organization celebrating its coming of age was the Women's Fellowship. I was asked to preach at the Thanksgiving Service in Wesley's Chapel, which was crowded for the occasion. I took as my text St Paul's words to the Philippians saying that he thanked God on every remembrance of the church in Philippi, which, as I reminded the congregation, had been founded by a group of women who met for prayer and who gave strong leadership to the church. I expressed my impatience with the way in which women's gifts were still not being fully used and recognized in the whole life and ministry of the Church. Too often we seemed to confine women's contribution to a domestic function. 'When any minister begins by saying, "Where would we be without the ladies?",' I suggested, 'we can guess what he will say next – he will thank them for making the tea! . . . While women are content to spend so much time in the church kitchens,' I went on to say, ' it's not surprising that so few of them are given any place in the church vestries.' My concern was not only for the ordination of women but for their full partnership with men in every part of the Church's life.

I suppose it was this concern that attracted the attention of Richard Kilburn, a BBC television producer who was preparing a documentary series for BBC2 called *Women, Women, Women*. It was intended to portray women who were living and working in 'a man's world'. I was chosen as the subject of a programme relating to the role of women in the Church. For ten days, therefore, I was accompanied everywhere I went by a team of cameramen, sound recording engineers and the production team. This somewhat bemused my audiences, particularly the 300 men gathered for the annual Laymen's Missionary Dinner at Westminster Central Hall, where a woman had never before been invited to speak.

One appointment I specially appreciated, though I found it a great challenge, was the invitation to give the William Ainslie Memorial Lecture at St Martin in the Fields. Its setting prompted me to expound some of the thoughts I'd absorbed through reading Harvey Cox's book, *The Secular City.* The very location of St Martin's, amidst the power centres of London, with South Africa House and Charing Cross station as its nearest neighbours, and the open public space of Trafalgar Square, seemed to illustrate the significant features of the modern, secular city – the politicians' power centre, the commuters' terminus, the forum for protest or celebration, with the church on the edge, sounding even by its name as though it belonged to a bygone age.

Yet St Martin's patron saint was the archetypal good neighbour, who sliced his coat in half to share with a beggar. I suggested that there might be a clue there as to one role of the Church within our modern society. I recalled the despicable election slogan that had been used during the campaign in Smethwick just a year before – 'Do you want a nigger for your neighbour?' For the Christian, I maintained, there is only one answer to that question: 'My neighbour is the person who is near me, anyone in need, and especially it is the ones who have fallen among the thieves of our society and who are battered by the blows of any kind of racial prejudice.'[2]

In all my addresses I found myself constantly drawing on my experience during the past year in New York. There was so much that seemed like dazzling success in the churches there – crowded congregations, professional ministries of men and women, generous resources. But the churches which had really impressed me were those that were attempting in a variety of ways to bridge the great gulf between the Church and the world in response to the

---

2  Pauline Webb, *Are We Yet Alive? Addresses on the Mission of the Church in the Modern World,* Epworth, 1966.

new and clamant needs of secular society. It was in one of the most prosperous, highly adorned churches in Manhattan that the minister, speaking to us visitors, had said:

> Though we stand here in the heart of the city we are separated from the world around us by a great gulf in that nothing we do really affects the life of all these great business houses and power centres. The only time most people beyond our membership make a move towards us from these huge apartment blocks is when in some kind of personal distress we throw a lifeline to them – a visit to a hospital, a funeral service, a word of comfort or counsel. How can this kind of crisis bridge ever bear the weight of the Church's involvement in the life of the world, or bear a real witness to our faith that God does indeed love this world , in its strength as well as in its weakness?

The dominant theme at the Methodist Conference itself was the whole question of Church unity and specifically of the Anglican–Methodist Conversations. In a crucial vote the Conference decided by an overwhelming majority to appoint a negotiating committee of twelve ministers and three lay people to meet with a similar group of Anglicans. Our job was to clarify points raised in the debate so far and to bring to the Conference of 1968 proposals for an actual scheme of union. The President himself was given the responsibility of nominating the negotiating group. I was both honoured and daunted by the proposal that I should be one of them, the only woman and the youngest member! The other representative of the younger generation was Geoffrey Ainger, one of the group ministry pioneering new work at Notting Hill.

During the next three years we met on six occasions, alternately on Methodist and Anglican premises. The Anglicans were able to invite us each time to meet in the imposing comfort of St George's

House, Windsor Castle, which made me conscious of the weight of the Establishment every time we drove through its massive gates! The debate centred particularly on the requirements of the Lambeth Quadrilateral, that any union must be based on Scripture, on the historic creeds, on the observance of the sacraments of baptism and holy communion and on the acceptance of the historic episcopate. It was on this last point that the debate was most prolonged. It went back to the days of John Wesley and the time of the American Revolution. Having tried in vain to persuade the Bishop of London to send clergy out to America in place of those who had come back to Britain out of loyalty to the crown, Wesley decided to send two of his preachers himself. As a presbyter he was not authorized to ordain, and in this way it was claimed that he had broken the uninterrupted tradition of episcopal ordination.

It was decided that the only way in which such a long separation between our two churches could be resolved would be through a Service of Reconciliation, in which it was hoped that it might be possible for the ministries of both our Churches to become mutually recognized, following a confession of penitence for our past division and making a commitment to our future unity. I remember Geoffrey Ainger commenting to me during one of our interminable debates, 'It feels rather like being at an El Alamein reunion, where old generals are still fighting the battles of faraway and long ago, and we want to cry out, "Come up, chaps! The war's over!"'

But it was by no means over. After the commission had issued its report (with a minority dissenting comment), we travelled up and down the country explaining, defending, commending its recommendations. In the end, although the scheme for union won a huge majority in the Methodist Conference it sadly failed to secure a large enough vote in the Anglican Synod to permit it to go any further forward. I recall that in our local parish church the vicar was so distressed by this failure that he flew a flag at half-mast and sent a letter of regret and repentance to be read to our Methodist congregation.

Meanwhile, we in the British Methodist Church were being wooed by our sister church on the other side of the Atlantic. They suggested that we should put our resources and energy into working out a scheme of closer union with the Conference of the United Methodist Church in the USA. Their ecclesiastical system was different from ours. They had their own form of episcopacy and in many ways our traditions had diverged. We were divided not by doctrine but by six thousand miles of ocean and two hundred years of history.

We agreed to the appointment of a representative body from our two churches to meet and explore the possibilities of closer liaison. Again, I was appointed as one of the representatives of British Methodism. Over three years we had three meetings, all in pleasant places – Boston, Bermuda and Geneva. To me it seemed a pointless exercise, an attempt at achieving painless ecumenism. We were in fact already in communion with one another. It is easy enough to unite with people of the same tradition on the other side of the world. The real challenge was to recognize our unity with Christians of different traditions from ours at the other end of the street!

Meanwhile, the World Methodist Council brought together in large gatherings every five years representatives of the 79 different churches of the Methodist family, embracing some 38 million members across the world, some of whom were now themselves part of united or uniting churches. The year of my Vice-Presidency was the year for their meeting in London. I was given responsibility for scripting an opening presentation for this large, jamboree-like gathering. Much influenced by satirical programmes like *That Was the Week, That Was* and *Beyond the Fringe* I wrote a revue-type programme called *Unwillingly to Aldersgate*, beginning with a well-worn quotation from John Wesley's diary describing how he went unwillingly to a meeting in Aldersgate Street. There, during the reading of Luther's Preface to the Epistle to the Romans, he had felt his heart 'strangely warmed'. At this point the actor playing John Wesley threw off his wig and wondered aloud how the great man would feel if he went to some of the Methodist churches across the world today. Each continent came in for its own strictures, and we who had presented the revue were by no means universally popular as a result!

Meanwhile the final report to the Methodist Conference of the Commission on Women and the Ministry was given at the end of my year as Vice-President. It was inconclusive, merely recommending continued discussion on the subject with the representatives of the Anglican Church. I responded by proposing that the Methodist Conference should now definitely affirm its conviction that women might properly be ordained to the ministry of word and sacraments, though we agreed it would be unwise to take unilateral action on this matter whilst union negotiations were in progress. I received strong support from the Revd Colin Morris, who was at the time the President of the United Church of Zambia and who had already himself ordained a Methodist missionary, Peggy Hiscock, as a woman minister in that church. Eileen Tresidder, a lay secretary in the Youth Department, also spoke in favour of the motion. The proposal won an overwhelming majority vote. When sadly the union talks eventually came to grief, at least the ordination of women in the Methodist Church was then able to proceed and the first women were ordained in 1974.

My greatest privilege came after my Vice-Presidential year was over. I was appointed to accompany the President to Kenya in order to sign the legal declarations granting autonomy to the Methodist Church of Kenya (which had previously been under the jurisdiction of the British Methodist Church). The Foundation

Conference was to be held on 9 January 1967. I was feeling tired after a year of over 20,000 miles of travelling across Britain, so I decided that immediately after Christmas I would take a few days' holiday on the way to Nairobi.

I flew first to Beirut, arriving there at sunset, with time for a quiet stroll through what seemed then a peaceful and elegant city, before spending the night in Hotel Bristol, ready for an early start at the airport the next morning. We flew low over Lebanon and had clear views of Galilee and Mount Hermon. I was met in Jerusalem by American friends, Bob and Vivien Bull, archaeologists, who took me to stay in their little home on the Mount of Olives. In the evening we went for a drive along the menacing road from Jerusalem to Jericho, down to the edge of the Dead Sea and then up to the Qumran caves, a journey to live in my memory for ever.

The next day they took me out to the site where they were working at Shechem. Bob pointed out to me the ruins of a city dating back to prehistoric times. At another site on Mount Gerizim, beneath the ruins of Hadrian's temple an older Samaritan temple was being excavated. It made Jesus' conversation with the Samaritan woman at the well come to life for me!

While Bob and Vivien got on with their work they left me to explore the holy sites in Jerusalem on my own, and I willingly suspended disbelief while guides made various claims about the sites (though I remained sceptical when the donkey-owner on the Mount of Olives assured me his animal was a direct descendant of the Palm Sunday ass! )

A greater thrill came when my hosts took me on a long journey through desert country, until we came suddenly upon the rose-red city of Petra, its buildings hewn out of rock, surely one of the great wonders of the world. I reluctantly had to leave the next day to continue my journey, which brought me to Cairo and the chance to see another of the world's wonders, the pyramids. Just spending one night there, two nights in Jerusalem and one in Beirut gave me an affection for the Middle East which has haunted me ever since as we've watched news film of destruction and violence there.

Eventually we arrived in the very different city of Nairobi with its broad streets and its white, colonial type buildings. Here I met up with the President of Conference again and we were given a wonderful, smiling welcome by the Revd Ronald M'gongo, the elected President of the new Kenya Methodist Church. The ceremony of signing the deed granting autonomy was held in the imposing Charter Hall, beautifully decorated with shields and pendants all in red, green and white, Kenya's national colours. There was a great sense of celebration and confidence.

The next day I had been appointed to preach at the Theological College in Limuru, a beautiful, simple building with blue décor and bright red falls on both the pulpit and lectern. The congregation comprised staff, students and a group of Sudanese refugees, many of whom told me they had walked for over 50 days to flee from the Sudan. I took as my theme, 'He has opened the doors of faith'.

The next day was the Foundation Conference itself where we were greatly impressed by the dignity of the induction ceremony of the new President, who gave his own personal testimony as to how he had come to faith in Christ. Then followed a 'Conversation on the Work of God', when I was much intrigued by watching the lively facial expression and gestures of an old man speaking in Swahili. I couldn't understand a word, except that I was sure by his body language that he was saying what old men all over the world say, 'Things aren't what they used to be!'

I was soon to realize that in this society old people are treated with great respect. But I did find it rather a shock when at one meeting the chairman, wanting to impress his audience by how important their visitors were, introduced me as 'a big, old woman' and the President as ' a decrepit old man'!

The most memorable part of this visit to Kenya was a journey out to the Mombasa Coast, where I had been invited to lay the foundation stone of a new school for physically disabled children which had been recently begun by one of the missionaries, Margaret Bridgewater. She had been prompted by the plight of so many disabled children with no means of support other than begging. The children were all excited to know that soon they would have their own school building. I found it moving when Dorka, one of the first pupils, stumbled up towards me on her two crutches to present me with a bouquet. I stretched out my hand to help her, but Margaret restrained me. 'No, let her walk by herself, however long it takes,' she said. Many years later I heard from Margaret that Dorka had grown up to become the school's most efficient secretary, having learned so early on to stand on her own feet.

As soon as we returned from Kenya I was due to take up a new appointment as Lay Training Director for the Methodist Church. No-one seemed quite sure what was expected of me in this post. Methodism had a long tradition of training lay preachers and Sunday school teachers and class leaders, but my own emphasis in everything I had said at Conference was on the role laymen and women should play, not just within the Church but beyond its walls in the world of work and of politics. I had heard of the Lay Academies in Germany and Holland and I had seen several interesting projects in New York, in which lay people were being encouraged to relate their faith to their professional and civic life as well as to their personal concerns. I dreamed of holding consultations and training courses on difficult ethical questions and work-related issues, helping people to think theologically about those matters that were of greatest concern to them in their weekday experience.

I had no premises other than an office in Chester House, the new building on the North Bank estate, opposite where I was then living in Muswell Hill. I had no staff other than a secretary with whom I worked out a possible timetable and filing system. And I had no resources except a small budget contributed and controlled by all the other interested departments, interested in making sure that I didn't tread on their territory!

So when the first Board of Lay Training met in the April of 1967 it had already become clear to me that this too would need to be an ecumenical undertaking. I was grateful to Anglican colleagues who were ready to share with me their own insights into varied forms of training, such as group sensitivity awareness and community development methods. I was also given enthusiastic support by a group of committed laymen, led by the economist Owen Nankivell and inspired by Mark Gibbs who had written about the laity as *God's Frozen People* and who was pleading for the churches to cease regarding their lay people as amateur or assistant clerics!

Yet a concern for world mission remained my major interest. I was always eager to emphasize that that word 'mission' needed redefining. As I said at a conference on 'New Directions in Mission' held in Cardiff: 'In every case we are being called to a right-about turn in thinking about mission and a turning inside-out of our church – but then nothing less than this can be expected when we fully explore the implications of a gospel which, it is claimed, can turn the world upside down.' There is so often in the concept of mission the arrogant assertion that one who has the light goes to take it to one who is in darkness – that mission means going from a Christian stronghold to a pagan place, hitherto unpenetrated by the love of God nor by the light of truth. Such a concept has surely been crushed by the crashing collapse of the idea of a Western

Christendom as the embodiment of the Kingdom of God called to extend its empire across the world. Mission has to be a giving as well as a receiving from others, so that in our shared experience we begin to discern the signs of the Kingdom which is already established among us all.

I was particularly glad to be invited to attend the meeting of the Overseas Consultation held at Hartley Victoria College in Manchester in July 1967. It was attended by a galaxy of leaders from churches overseas, including Daniel Niles from Ceylon, Bolaji Idowu from Nigeria and Hugh Sherlock from Jamaica, all of whom I had met personally during my travels. The main concern of the consultation was the end of anything like a colonial era of mission. These leaders were heads of autonomous churches who looked to London not for advice but for partnership. Among them was Colin Morris who five years before had written a book called *The End of the Missionary?* When we first published it we had made sure that there was a large question mark on the cover. It seemed that that question mark could now be removed altogether. The 'Missionary Society' changed its name and became known as the 'Overseas Division' of the Methodist Church, and missionaries themselves were eventually to be known as 'mission partners', working entirely under the direction of the churches to whom they were sent.

While the Church was changing its concept of mission the world seemed to be becoming more turbulent. In Britain, tighter immigration laws threatened to make entry to this country more and more difficult even for relatives coming to join people from overseas already living here. At the Women's World Day of Prayer in 1968, I said from the pulpit of St Martin in the Fields:

It would be sheer hypocrisy if women in Britain were to spend this day of prayer asserting their belief that they are called to bear the burdens of others and then go home to a 'backing little Britain' mentality which suggested that our concern ended at Dover . . . If there was ever a need in this country for people to think in human terms and with personal compassion it is at this moment when the hysterical amassing of figures and statistics can blind us to the faces of our fellow human beings.

Following this we drew up a positive affirmation for people to sign saying that they were ready and willing to live in a multiracial society and we invited people to come to St Martin's to sign it. Meanwhile, Enoch Powell played on people's fears by an inflammatory speech made in Birmingham in April 1968 against the growing number of immigrants and threatening people with the terrifying prophecy of rivers of blood flowing through the streets of Britain. In the same year two people who spoke words of hope to the world were silenced. Martin Luther King was assassinated on 4 April and shortly afterwards Robert Kennedy also fell victim to a gunman's bullet.

It was not only racial unrest that was tearing the world apart. Students in cities across the world were turning to protest. In Paris, screamed the newspaper headlines, 'Violence flares as the Sorbonne falls' and in London on the same day the press proclaimed 'Universities to crack down on British student revolutionaries'.

It was against this background that the Fourth Assembly of the World Council of Churches was convened in Uppsala and I was appointed to go as one of the eight representatives of the British Methodist Church. Little did I realize then that this was to be the beginning of another new chapter of my life.

# 6

## All Things New

❦

'Uppsala Ahoy!' proclaimed *Outlook,* the magazine of the Church Missionary Society, in its July 1968 issue. Beneath the headline was a cartoon depicting familiar faces of some of the delegates to the Fourth Assembly of the World Council of Churches, crammed together in one small boat en route for Uppsala. Among them were the Archbishops of both Canterbury and York (Ramsey and Coggan), Archbishop Iakovos of the Greek Orthodox Church, Dr Martin Niemöller of Germany, Bishop Kenneth Sansbury of the British Council of Churches and three of the few women elected by their churches – Christian Howard of the Church of England and Ruth Anstey and myself from the Methodist Church. It suggested that we were in for a perilous journey in this frail ecumenical vessel.

Certainly we were sailing into stormy waters. The world climate was one of student protests in Paris and London, race riots in Watts and Washington, war in Vietnam and civil strife between Nigeria and Biafra. Just two years earlier the WCC had held a Conference on Church and Society, calling for a New International Economic Order and acknowledging the revolutionary ferment among freedom movements in southern Africa. It seemed from the reports of that conference that the WCC was moving from a theology mainly concerned with Church order to a theology whose major emphasis was human liberation.

The Assembly began in great formality, with a distinguished

array of church dignitaries from all parts of the world, in varied ecclesiastical vestments processing into the ancient Swedish Lutheran cathedral of Uppsala: Orthodox patriarchs at the front, Anglican archbishops at the back, Protestant leaders somewhere in the middle. (It's always seemed to me a fortuitous ecumenical convenience that different churches have different ways of indicating precedence!) Then we were startled by the stuttering of trumpets in an ultra-modern setting of the introit which seemed to be warning us that in honouring our traditions we must also take seriously the cacophony of the contemporary world. Dr Daniel T. Niles preached the opening sermon, substituting for Dr Martin Luther King whose voice had been silenced by a gunman just a few weeks before. The sermon was on the theme of the whole Assembly, 'Behold! I make all things new'.

The plenary speeches in differing ways had a prophetic ring about them. The whole gathering withered under the blistering eloquence of black novelist James Baldwin, son of a pastor, describing himself as 'one of God's creatures whom the Christian Church has most betrayed'. His angry tirade was followed by the measured tones of Lord Caradon, the UK's representative at the UN, who linked the inequity of racism to the evils of world poverty. This in turn was followed by a long analysis of his own nation's economic problems by Kenneth Kaunda, President of Zambia. Just as we were all beginning to wilt under this welter of speeches the dynamic Lady Jackson (Barbara Ward) delighted and revived everyone (except the poor interpreters) by tearing up her manuscript and giving off the cuff one of the most witty, searching and memorable addresses of the whole Assembly. She warned us that unless we Christians woke up to our global responsibilities, by the end of the century we would be facing the prospect of world hunger and massive migration across the world of people seeking work and demanding their fair share of the world's depleting resources.

Throughout the Assembly there was brilliant use of modern media. We were frequently led in song by Pete Seeger, the popular American folk singer, who helped us celebrate the fact that 'We are black and white together' and to affirm our faith that 'We shall overcome'. In a powerful Swedish drama we heard Amos' repeated cry for justice. A film made for the assembly by John Taylor, working with Czech artists, depicted the dilemma of humanity facing the confusing demands of modern technology. And a BBC film presented a history of the Church seen from a secular point of view, highlighting the tragedy of our disunity.

The hardest work was done in five Sections. I was asked by Philip Potter to act as Secretary of the Section on Renewal in Mission, which meant that I had the nerve wracking responsibility of presenting that Section's Report to the whole Assembly. It contained particularly one new concern, the need for dialogue with people of other faiths: 'In dialogue,' we said, 'we discern our common humanity . . . As Christians we believe that Christ speaks in the dialogue, revealing himself to those who do not know him and correcting the limited and distorted knowledge of those who do.'

In the wake of the work in the Sections five new programmes were added to the WCC:

1  The Programme to Combat Racism.
2  The Commission on the Churches' Participation in Development, and a Joint Committee with the Vatican on Society, Development and Peace, known as SODEPAX.
3  The Christian Medical Commission.
4  Dialogue with people of living faiths and ideologies.
5  The sub-unit on Education.

The toughest part of the assembly came in the nominating of new presidents. There was a strong move on the part of the women delegates (who made up less than 9% of the total body) that there should be a woman President, there having been only one woman to hold this office, Sarah Chakko, since the formation of the WCC. That move however was defeated and once again an all-male praesidium was elected.

The fact that young people were not fully represented in the Assembly led to a revolt. Youth participants who were present were so angry that they took over the cathedral, where I joined in their protest as they locked themselves in there all night! When the Assembly gathered for its final service of dedication, the youth paraded through the cathedral armed with placards of the kind carried in political demonstrations, reminding the delegates of some of the solemn declarations made during the course of the proceedings.

The Assembly's final Message carried a ringing call to the churches:

> We heard the cry of those who long for peace, of the hungry and exploited who demand bread and justice, of the victims of discrimination who claim human dignity, and of the increasing millions who seek for the meaning of life . . . Christ wants his Church to foreshadow a renewed human community . . . Therefore we Christians will manifest our unity in Christ by entering into full fellowship with those of other races, classes, age, religious and political convictions in the place where we live.

The ecumenical movement, it seemed, had moved forward from the concept simply of Church unity to a concern for the unity of the whole of humanity. Catholicity was defined as 'the quality by which the church expresses the fullness, the integrity and the totality of life in Christ',

The purpose of Christ is to bring people of all times, of all races, of all places, of all conditions, into an organic and living unity in Christ by the Holy Spirit under the universal fatherhood of God.[1]

So, like most other people at Uppsala, I prepared to come home with a new world-wide vision of the *oikoumene,* which literally means a concern for the whole inhabited earth. But there was another shock in store for me. Having rejected the women's request for a woman to be elected as President, the new Central Committee (the main policy making body of the WCC), meeting immediately at the end of the Assembly, decided for the first time to appoint a woman officer, and to my stunned amazement I was told that they had elected me to be the Vice-Chairman (a title later changed, for obvious reasons, to Vice-Moderator). So a new world-wide responsibility was thrust upon me.

Thus I became a member of both the Central and Executive committees. Their meetings were held in various parts of the world and were intended to afford us opportunities not only to attend to the business of the Council between assemblies, but also to visit some of the member churches and to advocate its ecumenical concerns. During the seven years before the next assembly we met in 12 different countries. As an officer, I was also called to officers' meetings in Geneva. These included the Chairman, M. M. Thomas, a lay theologian from the Mar Thoma Church in South India, my co-Vice Chairman, Metropolitan Meliton of Chalcedon, who represented the Ecumenical Patriarchate, and the General Secretary, the Revd Eugene Carson Blake, an American Presbyterian. Meeting so often, sometimes in exotic places, meant that we became a close-bound team with a good pattern of working together. 'MM's own

---

1 Report on *The Holy Spirit and the Catholicity of the Church* presented at the Uppsala Assembly.

style of chairing was relaxed and informal, always trying to work towards consensus rather than decision by vote. When there was any particularly difficult debate in prospect he would ask me to chair and guide the proceedings according to accepted Western style rules of debate!

Our first Executive meeting took us to Oklahoma, right in the Bible belt of the USA. We were invited as guests of the Tulsa Ecumenical Council. Our opening service had been prepared and was led by a Roman Catholic layman. MM preached a sermon on the theme of Joy, full of ecumenical optimism. However we were soon made aware of the strength of the opposition of some of the more conservative churches in the area when we came under attack from an organization calling itself the International Council of Churches, which vehemently denounced the WCC, with its emphasis on international justice, as a 'communist' organization.

In the home where I was staying my hosts and I watched together a television debate between Philip Potter and one of these fierce critics of the WCC. My host commented, 'I'm not sure that I understand what the argument is all about, but I do recognize the Spirit of Christ when I hear it, and it seemed to me that that black guy (Philip) showed more of it than the man who was arguing with him.'

We were invited to dinner at the church of an American Indian congregation in Tulsa, where MM was delighted to be crowned with an Indian feather headdress, and made an honorary member of the Ponca tribe. 'I always wanted to be a *Red* Indian,' he joked.

A few months later I was called to Geneva to be one of the official party receiving Pope Paul VI, on his visit on 10 June 1969 to the Ecumenical Centre (Headquarters of the WCC). A closer relationship had for some time been growing between the WCC and the RC church. Inevitably the question was being raised as to whether the RC church would become a member church of the WCC. The

Pope's visit was looked forward to with great anticipation. I was teased about what I would wear and what I might say. One joker suggested I could ask, 'Do you come here often?' or even, 'Hello, Paul, I'm Pauline!'

I remember our long discussions before the visit about whether we could pray publicly together, for at that time it was still not accepted practice for Roman Catholics and Protestants to share in common prayer. It was finally decided that the WCC officers, together with the Pope, would engage in a time of silent, private prayer. This was regarded as such an unusual ecumenical event that *The Times* in London carried a front page photograph of the group of us praying silently, with heads bowed, in the chapel of the Ecumenical Centre. Then I was asked to open the proceedings in the main hall by reading a prayer of Pope John XXIII's and inviting everyone in the gathering to join in the Lord's Prayer, each in their own language. As I did so, I overheard an enthusiastic Canadian reporter whispering into his lip mike, 'This must be the first time in Church history that the Pope, the patriarchs, the bishops and the Protestant leaders have prayed publicly together as a family calling on God *our* Father.'

Both the Pope and Eugene Blake made courteous speeches of mutual good will, but neither suggested that there was any immediate prospect of there being any closer relationship. I remarked privately at the time that they reminded me of a coy couple who are being suspected of planning to marry, and who protest, 'No, we are just good friends'. You couldn't help feeling they were being driven together by a love so strong that they could not resist it. Certainly the wind of the Spirit was indeed to drive all the churches towards a closer relationship during the next 50 years. Shared prayer is nowadays a common feature of ecumenical gatherings.

Pope Paul, who seemed more relaxed as he went to celebrate

mass with his own faithful flock on the other side of Lake Geneva, invited our small group to join him in the boat crossing the lake. One of the guards on duty hesitated before allowing me, a woman, on board, but the Pope himself insisted on my sitting with him and we were even able to have a personal conversation in my broken French! I got the feeling that, reticent as he was, Pope Paul VI really did care deeply about the unity of the Church.

Very soon after the Pope's visit, I represented the officers at a special WCC-sponsored consultation on racism. This was called to explore ways of following up the recommendations from Uppsala, that there should be 'a crash programme to guide the Council and member churches in the matter of racism'. Ever since the time of its foundation the WCC had recognized racism as one of the greatest threats to the unity both of humanity and of the churches themselves. As J. H. Oldham had said in 1924, it is the duty of Christians not to explain racism but to end it.

By the 1960s, racism had developed into a major issue across the world. In South Africa it took its most ugly form in the brutal system of apartheid. The WCC had called its eight member churches in South Africa to a multiracial consultation at Cottesloe, where it had been declared that racism is totally incompatible with the gospel of Christ. The consultation's conclusions provoked such negative reactions in South Africa from both the government and the white Reformed churches that many of the churches withdrew from membership in the WCC.

At the Uppsala Assembly it had become clear that a world-wide programme was needed to combat racism not in words only but in actions that would speak more eloquently than any words. The WCC international consultation to prepare such a programme was held in Notting Hill and was chaired jointly by Senator McGovern of the USA and the Archbishop of Canterbury, Michael Ramsey. It was a stormy meeting, invaded at one point by black activists who, following what was happening in the USA, demanded that the churches pay large reparations to the people who had been wronged. As a kind of counterbalance, the public meeting held in the evening at Church House, where the speakers were Oliver Tambo and Trevor Huddleston, was interrupted by noisy, racist protests from white militant members of the National Front. The police were called, and I remember one American friend commenting to me that two things astonished her: first, that the police merely took the protestors by the arm and led them out, and secondly that the protestors left quietly!

The plan for a Programme to Combat Racism that eventually came out of the Consultation was presented at the Central Committee meeting in Canterbury in the summer of 1969. While it recognized that racism is a world-wide problem and takes many forms, it gave particular focus to white racism, associated as it is with power and wealth. A Special Fund would be launched to enable grants to be distributed to various organizations engaged in the struggle against racism, to express solidarity with them and trust in them.

Those of us on the Executive who supported the proposals for this Special Fund had a job persuading some of our fellow members to agree, but the proposals were brought to the floor of the whole Central Committee. There, after spirited debate, it was agreed that a Programme to Combat Racism be launched for an initial five-year period with the Dutch layman Boudewyn Sjollema as its Director working with a commission of people representative of racially oppressed groups across the world. As vice-moderator of the Central Committee, I was made a member of the commission and chaired its first meeting, where one of our members, Joyce Clague, an aborigine from Australia, and her husband Colin brought their two-week-old baby Anne Grace to be baptised, a sign of our hope for a non-racist future.

The first announcement of the grants allocated from the Special Fund was made at the next Executive meeting held the following autumn in Arnoldshain, West Germany. Among the recipients were FRELIMO, the liberation movement in Mozambique, once led by Edmund Mondlane, a committed Christian who had been killed shortly before he should himself have been present at the WCC Consultation on Racism. Grants were also allocated to SWAPO, the liberation movement in Namibia, whose cause was eloquently advocated in Britain by the exiled Anglican bishop, Colin Winter. The largest grants were to the ANC, whose leader, Nelson Mandela, was serving a life sentence in gaol, and to the PAC, also engaged in the struggle against apartheid in South Africa. Minor grants were made to racially oppressed groups in other parts of the world.

The announcement caused a furore in South Africa. The WCC was accused of supporting violence. The British press had a field day, with cartoons suggesting that church collections were being taken up by guerrillas in battle dress. Yet it was emphasized that the grants were specified as being for humanitarian and educational purposes and were given as a symbol of moral support for those who were the victims of violent racist regimes. The hope was that such support would make counter-violence unnecessary. To those who thought they had no voice left other than gunfire through which to make themselves heard in the world, the WCC was giving a voice in a non-violent action of tangible support for the oppressed. The principle was agreed that the WCC would trust the organizations receiving grants to use them as intended and not for the purchase of arms. There would be no paternalistic attempt to control their spending.

Opposition to the Programme to Combat Racism was widespread, particularly in Britain and in Germany. I personally received bags of mail from outraged correspondents who declared that the Church should never support those who were engaged in armed struggle. Most of the letters came not from pacifists but from people who had once fully supported our own armed forces. One such letter was signed Lt. Colonel (retd)! Having grown up in war-time myself, I had been taught that there were times when in the last resort, tragically, evil had to be resisted by force.

When our next Officers' meeting was due, Metropolitan Meliton invited us to be the guests of the Ecumenical Patriarchate in Istanbul, over what was their Easter weekend. We were met at the airport as VIP guests, but I was somewhat amused when the Patriarch's car, drawn up on the tarmac, whisked Gene Blake and MM off through the city, whilst I was conveyed behind in a tatty little taxi, it being deemed inappropriate for a woman to be seen as a passenger of the Patriarch!

Nevertheless I was received with great courtesy throughout the unforgettable Easter celebrations. I took part in the Good Friday procession in a packed church, where, in what looked like a tomb before us, the Gospel was placed to rest. We shared in the Easter vigil, when at midnight there rang out the words of the great Orthodox Easter acclamation – *Christ is risen! Risen indeed!* It echoed through the streets of Istanbul as the crowds came out from the church, carrying their lighted candles. Many people took up the refrain as they passed by.

On Sunday we went to the island of Halki where there is a School of Theology, and where we were given a superb Easter lunch. After returning by boat, MM and I went to see the once glorious Byzantine church, Hagia Sophia, which became a mosque for many years and was then converted into a museum. Its empty cavern was a gloomy sight, and MM and I talked together of how difficult but how important it is to affirm our resurrection faith in the face of such evident decay and defeat.

Having shared in the celebrations of an Orthodox Easter I found it an equally memorable experience to be in Ethiopia at the time of Timkat, the Coptic Orthodox Festival of the Epiphany. Our second Central Committee was held in Addis Ababa at the time of Epiphany 1971. The state and the Church in Ethiopia went to great pains to act as our hosts and the Emperor Haile Selassie took a personal interest in our presence. The committee began with an impressive service in the cathedral, when for the first time I became used to hearing the rhythmic chanting of the Coptic liturgy, which I have enjoyed again on many subsequent visits to the Coptic Orthodox Church in London.

In his Chairman's report MM made the challenging assertion that ecumenism required of all of us a transcending of our own ecclesiastical traditions in order to explore together a fuller relationship with Christ as Lord. My mind was stretched even further by the masterly address from Metropolitan Kodhr of the Greek Orthodox Church on the theology of inter-faith dialogue, as he spoke of this dialogue as being dependent on the work of the Spirit and not being confined only to those who claim to know the Son.

The Timkat Festival was a joyous, colourful celebration for the whole city. We were included in the great procession through the streets with placards commemorating the baptism of Christ. The Emperor himself was sprinkled with water, in a re-enactment of his own baptism and soon everyone else was following suit. It was a privilege to be the guest of the Emperor at a prayer breakfast held in the imperial palace. Small as he was in stature, he had an awesome presence. I was seated at the top table among other members of the royal family, still then enjoying a grandeur which was soon to be demolished.

The most tense debate in the Central Committee itself was the debate on the Programme to Combat Racism which was having repercussions all over the world. Present in the committee was John Rees, General Secretary of the South African Council of

Churches, who spoke briefly about the angry reaction in South Africa to the news of the grants made to the ANC and the PAC. He accepted a suggestion that a dozen South African representatives should come to Geneva for a conversation on racism with representatives of the WCC. However, after a long debate the PCR was endorsed with none voting against but with three abstentions, all incidentally from delegates of UK churches

\*   \*   \*

As had become the custom between us, MM asked me to chair this particularly intense debate, in which I managed, with difficulty, to be strictly neutral and was generously congratulated by both opponents and supporters of the programme. But I confess that I was so exhausted by it all that after it was over I crept off to my room for a good weep!

I was looking forward then to a holiday. Theo Kotze, a South African Methodist minister who had become a good friend of mine when he was speaking some years before at a conference at Swanwick in Derbyshire, had invited me to come to South Africa to stay with him and Helen his wife, and to preach at his church. It was an entirely private arrangement so when I arrived at Johannesburg airport I confidently presented my British passport. Then it was immediately taken from me and I was told to stand aside whilst the rest of the queue of departing passengers went off, some looking askance at me, wondering whether perhaps I had some infectious complaint! I was then escorted under police guard to a small waiting room and told that I would not be allowed to enter the country but must return to the UK on the next available flight. It took some hours before any such arrangement could be made and I was not meanwhile allowed to communicate with anyone outside. I knew that another Methodist minister, the Revd

Brian Brown, was waiting at the airport to meet me, but he was refused any news of what had happened, being told only that I had boarded the plane but not landed. He suggested that this implied some carelessness on the part of the airline, but no-one seemed to know what had happened to me.

Eventually when it became clear that there was no plane until the next day, I thought at first I was going to have to stay in the airport. However I was told that I could stay overnight in a nearby hotel, on condition that I spoke at no public meeting and gave no interview to the press. I was also told that I was now *persona non grata* in South Africa and would not be allowed entry if I ever attempted to come there again.

Brian Brown fortunately had patiently waited for me and so he was able to take me to a hotel. Within a few moments of my arriving there I had a phone call from C. F. Beyers Naudé. He was himself Afrikaans and had been a former Moderator of the Dutch Reformed Church. He had been discharged from the ministry when he took up Directorship of the Christian Institute, a body committed to opposition to apartheid. He invited me to his home for dinner, and said he would come and fetch me himself. He was sure we would be followed, but he was prepared to take that risk.

So I was privileged to spend the evening in an elegant home. Beyers's wife Ilse was a most gracious hostess. Everything in the room was tasteful and pleasant. Yet I felt around us a sense of impending danger. Beyers put on a record of classical music while we dined by candlelight. He explained to me that this was not just for entertainment but to prevent our conversation being overheard as he was sure his home was bugged. He wanted to hear all about the policy and strategy adopted by the Programme to Combat Racism. I was immediately reminded of a film I'd seen long ago, before the war. It was called *The Mortal Storm* and showed how a German professor and his wife were trying to maintain the usual courtesies of a civilized life while all around them was the menacing approach of a barbaric regime.

After we had discussed the politics of the situation in South Africa, and the debate that the Programme to Combat Racism was sure to provoke in the churches there, we went on to share some of the spiritual implications of the whole struggle against the evil of racism, and before I left we had a time of prayer and fellowship together. My friendship with the Naude's became a lifelong one, though I was never able to visit them again until not long before Beyers died in 2004. It was fitting that in the new South Africa this courageous churchman was given the honour of a state funeral.

Before going back to London I was asked to call at the WCC Headquarters in Geneva to report to the staff there on what had happened. I told them that the officials in South Africa said a letter had been sent to me warning me that I would not be welcome in South Africa, but no such letter had ever arrived. It seemed certain that no-one closely associated with the Programme to Combat Racism or even with the World Council of Churches would now be allowed into South Africa.

On my arrival back in Britain I was met by television cameras and whisked off to a press interview room at Heathrow airport. The *Guardian* headlined the story, 'Church official expelled' and, as it happened, on the same front page reported that the Anglican Dean of Johannesburg, the Very Revd Gonville ffrench-Beytagh, had just been released on bail after being arrested for his anti-apartheid protests. There was obviously some truth in what an official at the British Consulate in Johannesburg had said to me when I appealed for his help: 'The churches seem to be causing a lot of trouble here these days!'

I was relieved to be home, but troubled to find my mother displaying the first signs of confusion caused by Alzheimer's disease. The TV news had carried the story of my expulsion from South

Africa, and she became convinced that I must have been in some terrible danger, so we had to reassure her that I was now home safe and sound.

This was the beginning of a time of considerable anxiety at home. My parents had recently moved down to the coast and my two sisters and I took it in turns to go down there to care for them. My mother's health was rapidly deteriorating. So eventually she and my father came back up to London and stayed in my flat where I could keep an eye on them both. Fortunately my flat was close to Chester House, where my office as Director of Lay Training was based.

I was coming near to the end of my term in this experimental job. We had held some good lay conferences, and I had been travelling far round the circuits encouraging lay people to take a greater interest in the concerns of the communities in which they worked or lived. We had held some stimulating lay consultations at North Bank, the country house next door to Chester House on the estate at Muswell Hill. We had even invited a most enthusiastic team of people from the Chicago Ecumenical Institute to come and introduce some of their methods of lay training, which proved somewhat high-powered for our more laid-back British participants! We set up several projects across the country to encourage lay people to think theologically about current issues or their professional concerns, but it was difficult to get rid of the generally held concept of a 'lay' person as a kind of amateur or assistant cleric. Having worked in the WCC in such close colleagueship with M. M. Thomas, one of the finest lay theologians I have known personally, it seemed to me that the Church as a whole needed to work out more thoroughly a theology of the laity as the *laos*, the people of God with their own particular insights and forms of mission in the world.

It was just at this time that it was becoming possible for women to offer for the Methodist ministry and some of my friends thought that, having campaigned for that for so long, I would be one of the first to offer. But partly my increased responsibilities in my home situation and partly my growing awareness of the part that lay people had to play in both Church and society seemed to diminish the sense of call I once had, particularly to the ordained ministry.

At home my mother's deepening dementia meant there was a reversal of roles between us. She who had been such a strong, dependable parent now became as dependent as a child on my sisters and me and we in turn took on the role of parent. So many of the menial tasks she had once performed for us we now needed to perform for her. There were times when she didn't know where she was or even who we were. Just as her first act of love towards us had been to provide us with nourishment in a warm embrace, so now our last act of love towards her was to feed her with her favourite food and to enfold her in loving arms. We were rewarded in the end with a farewell smile. It was a smile of hope, for we believed, as she believed, that death was not the end but a new beginning.

I too now faced a new beginning. I was invited to return to the Methodist Missionary Society (known now as the Overseas Division) as an Area Secretary, responsible for relations with the churches in what was called the 'western area', which included West Africa, Europe, the Caribbean and Latin America. So clearly my travelling days were by no means yet done!

# 7

# *Break Down the Walls*

**M**y travel diary over the next few years was exceptionally crowded. This was not only because of the responsibilities of my new job but also because of my many ecumenical duties while I continued to be an officer of the World Council of Churches. I found it remarkable that, in a Europe rigidly divided by a mythical iron curtain and by an actual dividing wall, leaders of Christian churches were still able and eager to meet one another across all the political barriers. Inevitably there was some mutual suspicion as to how those who came to meetings from Eastern Europe were free to travel when so many of their fellow citizens were severely restricted. Aware of the hardship and even persecution endured by some Christians living in totalitarian, atheist regimes we knew we had to respect the constraints of a fellowship which did not probe into the current propaganda so deeply as to endanger the lives of others or to make ecumenical contact impossible. For many of our colleagues in Eastern Europe, the World Council of Churches opened doors to the fellowship of the world-wide Church from which they would otherwise have been isolated.

Almost immediately after we had taken up office at the end of the Uppsala Assembly, the Russian military intervention in Czechoslovakia in August 1968 prompted us as officers of the WCC to issue a statement in protest. Patriarch Alexis of Moscow and all Russia, together with the Metropolitan of Warsaw and all

Poland, immediately sought to justify the Russian action as supporting the people by defending them against the destruction of socialism. We replied by saying that though we accepted their criticism of our statement 'in the spirit of ecumenical fellowship' we reiterated our hope that the troops would soon be withdrawn and normal international relations be restored.

I was particularly grateful for the opportunities given me personally to penetrate the so-called 'Iron Curtain' when we were invited to hold our Executive Committee meeting in 1971 in Sofia, Bulgaria. I was able to welcome there the woman who had at last been nominated as a President of the WCC, Dr Kiyoko Cho, from the United Church of Christ in Japan. She had been chosen by Eugene Blake to fill the vacancy caused by the untimely death of the renowned Asian leader and preacher at the Uppsala Assembly, Dr Daniel T. Niles.

During the meeting we enjoyed the lavish hospitality which is typical of the Orthodox tradition. We attended a magnificent three-hour long service in the ornate cathedral of Sofia, we visited the Rila monastery and we were guests at a sumptuous reception given by the Orthodox Patriarch. By the end of the dinner, I was shocked to receive a pencilled note from Dr Blake, saying, 'Will you please do the speech of thanks, as I think you may be the only person still sober? In German please!' I confess my German is only rudimentary and school-learnt, but so responsive was that audience that my every remark, whether intended to be amusing or not, was greeted with hilarious laughter and applause. Our hosts invited us to spend our last two days relaxing on the golden beaches of the Black Sea, which were crowded with holiday makers.

Early the next year we were again indebted to Orthodox hospitality. We were scheduled to meet for the next Executive in New Zealand. The Russian Orthodox Church offered to pay our fares for the whole journey, provided we travelled via Moscow. I believe this was by way of compensation for the fact that due to currency regulations the Church was not permitted to pay directly the full contribution due from a member Church of the WCC. So, accompanied by the Earl of March, who had become Chairman of the WCC Finance Committee, and Dr Ernest Payne of the Baptist Union, I travelled by Aeroflot to Moscow where we were given a VIP welcome and driven off in a posh-looking car to Hotel Russia, the largest hotel, we were told, in the whole of Europe.

I found Moscow an impressive city with an almost total lack of advertisement hoardings and neon lights. Its shops were inconspicuous and had little choice to offer – it was certainly not a consumer-oriented society. A day of sight-seeing in the city was carefully planned for us. We were not sure whether it was deliberate or not but we were not left at all to explore on our own. We saw in the Kremlin the magnificent treasures from Russia's past now housed in cathedrals turned into museums, but carefully preserved, not at all like our 'ruins that Cromwell knocked about a bit'. It struck me that it was as though Russia had pickled its heart.

A two-hour ride out of Moscow took us to the monastery and theological college at Zagorsk. At lunch, I sat next to the State Minister of Religion who was himself a Christian. When I expressed concern that the church should be under state control, he pointedly asked me who actually appointed our bishops and I launched into a long, historical explanation of church–state relations in Britain.

On Sunday we worshipped in the cathedral, in a congregation of well over 4000. We were told this was one of 50 churches in Moscow still holding regular services.

From there we went straight to the Baptist Church which again was overcrowded, though it was the third service of the day. Dr Payne, Dr Blake and I were invited into the pulpit, so we had a wonderful view of the congregation whose intense concentration and work-worn faces were worthy of an oil painting. There were over 70 young people in the choir, who sang many Russian hymns and some familiar Moody and Sankey ones. Two generations of atheistic education seemed to be having little effect on them! It was moving to share in the Communion service. Five huge loaves of bread and twelve chalices were passed round with difficulty among the whole congregation packed tight on the pews, in the aisles and on the staircases.

Our long journey on to New Zealand took us via New Delhi and Bangkok, arriving eventually in Singapore where we changed to New Zealand airlines for the flight to Auckland. A mixed reception was awaiting us. On the one hand, representatives of the National Council of Churches, including women and young people, greeted us with bouquets and embraces; but just behind them stood a group of protestors with placards proclaiming, 'Away with the WCC – agents of Communism – betrayers of the gospel!' To my surprise I recognized among the protestors an old friend – the big, black bishop who had been one of our ecumenical group in New York! I instinctively went up to embrace him affectionately, a gesture that was captured by the TV cameras who had gathered around us. So that evening this made headline news on television when I was undeservedly credited with setting an example of how one could deflect criticism by meeting it with friendship!

Among the New Zealand churches themselves we met nothing but enthusiasm for this first visit of an international WCC delegation to that part of the world. At the welcome meeting in Auckland Town Hall, all 2000 seats were filled. We were given a rousing Maori welcome, to which one of our Presidents, Bishop Zulu, made an eloquent response. I was the first of three main speakers. I tried specifically to address the issue that was causing so much controversy in the press and in the Western churches, the

Programme to Combat Racism. I spoke of the motivation behind the Special Fund, its methods of giving support to the racially oppressed, and the message it was seeking to communicate – that racism is totally incompatible with the gospel of Jesus Christ.

In our committee meeting we were faced with news of a worsening situation in Rhodesia. Violence had erupted when the Pearce Commission was sent out by the British Government to test public reactions to Anglo-Rhodesian plans for independence. Ian Smith, who had declared unilateral independence in 1970, had ordered the police to break up riots when the Commission visited the city of Gwelo. One man was shot dead, others were injured and Garfield Todd, the former Prime Minister, and his daughter Judith who lived in the area were both imprisoned. Garfield, a former missionary and teacher, had lived in Rhodesia for over 30 years and had always been a staunch upholder of the rights of Africans. He had been present with us in Notting Hill at the WCC's Consultation on Racism. I was given the job of drawing up a public statement expressing our condemnation of Ian Smith's action and pledging our active and prayerful support for Garfield and Judith.

Following our work in the committee, we all went to address various gatherings on the northern island, including one where Dr Cho and I addressed a conference attended by some 700 women. We were sent to different churches to preach, to enlarge our own ecumenical experience. Professor Sabev, from the Orthodox Church in Bulgaria, preached in a Salvation Army citadel, while Metropolitan Nikodim, Russian Orthodox, preached to Methodists, one of whom commented to me afterwards in surprise, 'His preaching was soundly biblical!' I had the privilege of preaching in St Thomas' Anglican Church, where I was allowed to sit in the chair used by Bishop Selwyn, the first bishop to work in New Zealand 100 years ago.

After a tour of Auckland's impressive harbour surrounded by

volcanic mountains, we flew to the South Island, and thence to Christchurch, which is like a little bit of England set in a tropical climate. Amid a full programme of appointments there, the most memorable for me was in a small coastal town called Oamaru where I chose to tell the story of Garfield Todd, quoting him as a man who had carried his personal faith into the political world and had given a courageous, though costly, Christian witness. Only at the end of the meeting was I told that Oamaru was Garfield's home town and that his sister was present in the meeting!

It was a long journey back to Christchurch, where I had another couple of preaching appointments before leaving for Australia. Between us, following our committee meeting, members of the Executive had addressed during our time in New Zealand over 200 gatherings, as well as giving innumerable interviews for radio, press and television. After a short stay in the International House in Sydney and a flying visit to Adelaide where I preached at the great Methodist City Mission, I caught the plane for the long journey back home.

The next few months were extraordinarily demanding. I had increased domestic responsibilities, I needed to reflect on my chequered years of experience in the Lay Training experiment and I wanted to prepare for my next job in the Overseas Division. Meanwhile the controversy over the Special Fund of the Pro-gramme to Combat Racism (PCR) was unabated. On a variety of occasions I had to defend the decision to give aid to the liberation movements and to other groups of racially oppressed people. I was challenged to a debate in the Oxford Union and subjected to a hard-hitting interview on TV with the formidable controversialist, Malcolm Muggeridge. The PCR was put 'on trial' in a BBC radio programme called *You the Jury* in which I was the defendant and the Revd George Austin, an Anglican priest and friend of South Africa, was the prosecutor. Before the broadcast I sought advice from the exiled South African lawyer, Albie Sachs (now Justice Sachs of the Constitutional Court of South Africa). His advice surprised me. He said, 'Don't try to remain calm throughout the debate. Let people see how angry you are about the suffering caused by the injustice of the anti-apartheid regime.' His advice proved effective and the World Council of Churches and its Programme to Combat Racism were exonerated from all accusation of guilt by the vote of the studio audience.

Many of my preaching appointments were disrupted by hecklers who seemed unable or unwilling to recognize that a concern for racial justice has its roots in the Bible and not in any communist manifesto. Fortunately, the Methodist Church Overseas Division had consistently supported the PCR, like an increasing number of ecumenical groups and churches particularly in the Netherlands and in the Federal Republic of Germany.

After the initial shock caused by the announcement of the grants made from the Special Fund, the attack on racism moved into an even more vulnerable area. The next target of the PCR became the investments by which the whole economy in South Africa was supported. At first there were those who argued that constructive engagement in the South African economy could be a way of bringing about reform. This was a line of argument which many Church investors doggedly pursued when we first suggested they re-examine their investment portfolios and ask how far they were by financial support upholding an iniquitous system of oppression. In the Commission of the Programme to Combat Racism we came to two major ethical decisions: first to call for total disinvestment in southern Africa and second to call on banks to cease granting loans to the South African government. The World Council of Churches screened its own portfolio and sold its shares in multinational companies operating in the countries concerned. It also drew up a list of all banks participating in loans to South Africa.

Here in Britain those of us who supported the PCR pleaded the cause of disinvestment with the finance committees of the major churches, the Church Commissioners and the British Council of Churches. Under the leadership of the Revd David Haslam, who was at the time minister of my own local Methodist church, we began a campaign against the banks called End Loans to South Africa. We used many different methods of making our point, engaging in street theatre, distributing leaflets to customers and employing shareholder action by presenting resolutions at the banks' annual meetings.

The debate about investment and bank loans came to a head in the next meeting of the WCC Central Committee held at Utrecht in August 1972. Representatives of some of the multinational companies came to Utrecht to lobby members of the Central Committee, trying to persuade them that the people who would suffer most as the result of such a boycott policy would be black people themselves, through the massive unemployment that would result. But the WCC, the South African Council of Churches and many of the African Church leaders, including Desmond Tutu, saw the policy of disinvestment and the ending of financial support as a vital last attempt to bring about non-violent change in South Africa. The Central Committee finally opted for the radical approach of withdrawal of investment. The WCC's naming of corporations directly investing in or trading with southern Africa put pressure on all member churches to check their portfolios and in some cases to start shareholder action. The discussion this subsequently provoked within the churches on the whole subject of investment ethics led eventually in Britain to the setting up of EIRIS, the Ethical Investment Research and Information Service.

I learned through all these debates what an eloquent symbol money has become. It seemed ironic that on the one hand people complained bitterly about our making funds available to meet the humanitarian needs of the oppressed struggling to make their voices heard in the world, while on the other hand the same people found it unacceptable that money should be withdrawn from businesses and banks profiting from exploitative and discriminatory practices. When we launched the Special Fund we had said that we needed an action that would speak louder than any words. It certainly seemed that by our 'putting our money where our mouth was' people did hear the message we were trying to convey. I found myself often quoting the words of Jesus, 'Where your treasure is, there will your heart be also'.

The other major decision made at the Utrecht Central Committee was the election of a new General Secretary to succeed Eugene Blake who had announced his intention to retire. I had been a member of the nominating committee, whose final meeting was in secret conclave just outside Utrecht. I made little secret of what I hoped would be the outcome as we discussed four possible candidates. It seemed to me that the hand of God was resting on Philip Potter who, from the time of his presence as leader of the youth delegation at the first Assembly of the WCC in Amsterdam, had shown visionary enthusiasm for the ecumenical movement combined with gifts of oratory, scholarship and total dedication to Christ and the Church. It seemed an added bonus that he would be the first General Secretary to come from the so-called 'third world'. When his name was finally brought to the Central Committee it won universal acclaim and he was unanimously elected.

Philip's responsibility in the WCC prior to his election as General Secretary had been as Director of the Commission on World Mission and Evangelism. It was in that role that he had planned and now steered through the momentous Conference on Salvation Today held in Bangkok in 1972. Of all the words used in the language of faith, 'salvation' is surely one of the most difficult to define. The apparently simple question of the street corner evangelist, 'Are you saved?' may prompt a number of different responses. 'Saved *from* what? Saved *for* what? Saved by whom, and when – in the past, present or future?' (All of these tenses are used significantly in the New Testament.) The aim of the Bangkok Conference was to explore the full meaning of this word which has too often been relegated to the language of religious discourse and robbed of any secular relevance.

As preparation for the conference an anthology was published of contemporary writings drawn from a variety of cultures all expressing a search for some kind of salvation. At the Bangkok gathering itself, people coming from 60 different nations gave their definitions of the word used for 'salvation' in their own languages and sought to express what they saw as the urgent need of their own peoples. Beginning with such contemporary concerns, Hans-Ruedi Weber, who held the portfolio of Biblical Studies at the WCC, took us deep into the biblical understanding of 'salvation history'. He began with the Exodus story and then on through the gospel of Christ's sacrificial love displayed on the cross to the final victory shouts of 'Salvation to God' in the Book of Revelation. Philip Potter himself, with his customary love of etymology, unpacked the meaning of the Biblical Greek, Latin and Hebrew terms for salvation. He defined it as being liberated *from* all that impedes our true humanity – sin, rebellion against God, enmity – *for* all that makes for well-being, outward and inward – in the community and in our personal and spiritual experience.[1]

Among the participants in the Bangkok Conference were people who lived in situations of conflict whom we had specifically invited to discuss what salvation could mean in their context. Accompanying me was a shy young woman from Northern

---

1  Pauline Webb, *Salvation Today*, SCM Press, 1974, pp. 7–9.

Ireland, where the 'troubles' between Loyalists and Republicans, often loosely identified as Protestants and Catholics, were coming to their height. She was Mairead Corrigan, a Roman Catholic, who was at first a bit intimidated at the thought of attending her first international gathering. She was later to become well known as a co-founder of the widely acclaimed Northern Ireland Peace Movement (later renamed Community of Peace People) and was one of those awarded the Nobel Peace prize.

Peace, justice, freedom – all these were cited at the Bangkok conference as the outworking of salvation in response to the needs of contemporary society. General Booth, founder of the Salvation Army, had once said, 'Soup, soap and salvation all belong together!' – in other words, those who care for the needs of the soul must care for the needs of the body too. Similarly, those who are concerned for the salvation of the individual person must be concerned for the salvation of the whole of society too.

The exotic beauty of our surroundings in the Red Cross Centre outside Bangkok where we were meeting and the grace of our Thai hosts who entertained us with their traditional dance and singing created a soothing air of tranquillity. Otherwise the conference could have become obsessed with the troubles of the world around us, particularly the war raging not far away from us, in Vietnam. Some even suggested we should go personally and place ourselves in the line of fire there, as a symbolic gesture of the sacrifice that salvation requires. There had been no shortage of statements by church leaders, including the leaders of American churches, protesting against this war. To this the Bangkok Conference added its own comment:

How can we preach the good news of Salvation Today, when on the same day a holocaust of destruction is unleashed which is widely believed by its perpetrators to be a defence of freedom and Christian values?[2]

The Bangkok Conference was for me and for many a stimulating challenge to strenuous theological thinking. In the study group I was asked to chair, the secretary was a German theologian by name Jürgen Moltmann, whose books I confess I had not then read, but which I have never missed since! He taught us to think with the realism that recognizes the power of evil, but to live with the optimism that acknowledges the power of grace.

So it was with hope in our hearts that we in Bangkok celebrated the dawn of a new year. Having lit each other's candles, we processed through the surrounding gardens, singing together the words that had become the theme song of our conference, 'Go down Moses and let my people go!'

The year 1973 marked the Silver Jubilee of the WCC. It was appropriate, though unplanned, that the Central Committee met in Geneva instead of in Helsinki where it had originally been scheduled. For me personally it was a sad journey, as when I arrived in Geneva, Philip broke to me the news that my beloved father, who had been ill and whom my sister was nursing at her home in Tonbridge, had died just after I had visited him and left for the airport. The family had tried to contact me at Heathrow but it was too late as I was on my way, so they phoned Philip instead. I couldn't have been surrounded by more comfort and support than I received from this group of friends from so many different confessions and parts of the world. I thought how moved my father would have been to have heard the prayers offered for him and for my family by Metropolitan Nikodim of Russia in the chapel of the Ecumenical Centre. It seemed particularly appropriate, as my

---

2  Pauline Webb, *Salvation Today*, SCM Press, 1974, pp. 78.

1  Students at King's College, London, 1946;
l Pamela Watts (later Paul), r Pauline Webb

2  Talking to young people about world issues, 1953

3 'The angry young woman' featured in the *Daily Sketch*, 1957

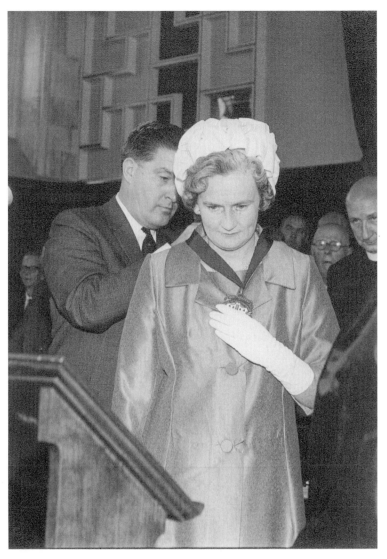

4  Being inducted by Douglas Brown as Vice-President of the Methodist Conference, 1965

5 Reading to my godson John Myers, 1966

6 The Pope's visit to the Ecumenical Headquarters, Geneva, 1969;
l–r P.W. (Vice-Chair WCC), M. M. Thomas (Chairman), Metropolitan Meliton
(Co-Vice-Chair), Pope Paul VI

7 Celebrating my parents' Golden Wedding with my sisters Muriel and Joy, 1970

8 Commission members of the WCC Programme to Combat Racism, 1970; seated l–r P.W., Baldwin Sjollema, Joyce Clague, standing l–r In Ha Lee, Jose Chipenda, Nawaz Dawood, Gonzalo Castillo-Cardenas

9 Guests of Haile Selassie, Emperor of Ethiopia, WCC Central Committee, 1971

10 Christian Campaign Against Racism and Fascism, Hyde Park, 1978

11  Opening worship of 6th Assembly of the WCC, Vancouver, 1983; l–r Archbishop of Canada (Rt Revd E. Scott), Revd Dr Philip Potter, P.W.

12  Welcoming Bishop Desmond Tutu's delayed arrival in Vancouver, 1983

13  Producing *Reflections* for BBC World Service with the Archbishop of
Canterbury, Most Revd Robert Runcie, 1984

14  *Reflections* with Cardinal Basil Hume, 1984

15  Filming on location for *Songs of Praise*, 1987

16  Recording *Songs of Praise* with villagers in Zimbabwe, 1987

17 Members of my local Methodist church at Harlesden, 1997

18 Congratulating my 'son in the gospel' Robert Maginley and his wife Shirley after Robert's ordination at St Margaret's, Westminster, 1997

19 Meeting again the veteran anti-apartheid prophet and pastor, the Revd Dr Beyers Naudé, in Johannesburg, 2000

20 Welcoming former President Nelson Mandela as guest speaker at the 8th Assembly of the WCC in Harare, 1998

sisters and I were divided on matters of faith. My elder sister, Joy, had become a Roman Catholic, whilst Muriel had remained a staunchly conservative Methodist. But my father's constant, equal love for all three of us had held us together as a family, which was a kind of ecumenical parable in itself.

A great ecumenical service was held in the Cathedral of St Pierre to celebrate the Silver Jubilee of the WCC. It was led by Visser 't Hooft, the doughty Dutchman who had kept the ecumenical vision alive throughout the years of the Second World War. Having kept in touch with church leaders on both sides of the conflict he had been the main architect of the structure of the Council and particularly of its first Assembly at Amsterdam in 1948. Sharing the service with him was Eugene Blake, the American who had succeeded 'Vim' as General Secretary. The present General Secretary, Philip Potter, was the preacher.

In the Central Committee meeting itself I was invited to be one of a panel of speakers reflecting on what the ecumenical movement had meant in my own experience. I spoke of the keen disappointment some of us had felt in Britain over the failure of the Scheme for Anglican–Methodist Union and how particularly sad and significant it seemed to me that the stumbling block for some people came in the requirement to engage in a service of reconciliation which would have acknowledged fault on both sides and made possible a sign of mutual forgiveness. We looked to church union schemes in other parts of the world to help us to find a way forward.

The Programme to Combat Racism was not much debated this time, though a delegation from the South African churches was present in the meeting. The study which now began to draw attention was one on 'Violence and non-violence in the struggle for social justice' which pointed out that the choice may not always be between violence and non-violence, but between engagement and non-engagement in the struggle for justice. So often there is violence on both sides.

We were beginning to make plans for the next Assembly, which so far had been scheduled to be held in Djakarta, Indonesia. It was decided that the theme would be 'Jesus Christ Frees and Unites'. A small group of us was particularly concerned about another issue concerning liberation and partnership which we wanted to see coming more prominently on to the agenda of the WCC. This was the question of the participation of women, who were at the time grossly under-represented both on the staff and on the ecumenical committees. We could see that unless drastic steps were taken women would once again be a minority presence in the Assembly itself.

As chair of the staffing committee, I tried but failed to persuade the Executive that until the time of the next Assembly all WCC staff vacancies should where possible be filled by women. The WCC had from its earliest days been served by some distinguished women on its staff, such as the inspiring teacher and leader of Bible study at Bossey, Suzanne de Dietrich. At the administrative and secretarial level the WCC had reason to be grateful for the dedicated service of many skilled women, but the programme staff remained pre-dominantly male. Much ecumenical initiative across the world was due to the influence of women, through movements like the Women's World Day of Prayer, the Fellowship of the Least Coin (founded in Asia) and the YWCA. Yet when it came to the question of how member churches chose their delegations to the assembly women were still very much in the minority.

At the next Executive meeting, we spent long hours trying to hammer out a staffing policy which would ensure a greater turn around of staff and a more diverse mixture of nationalities and of gender. We introduced what became an unpopular 'nine-year rule' decreeing that staff appointments should be for a maximum period of nine years. The hope was that staff would then be prepared to return to their home countries both to enrich the ecumenical experience within their own nation and also to enable new talent to be nurtured in the WCC. Among former members of the WCC staff who had returned after exile to give distinguished service in their own lands were Desmond Tutu, who had worked in the London office of the Theological Education Fund, and Paulo Freire, the renowned Brazilian educationalist.

The Executive was held in what might also be described as being 'behind the iron curtain', in East Germany, still known as the DDR (German Democratic Republic). We were guests at Bad Sarrow, a delightful spa in the snow-covered countryside. From there we went out to address several congregations of people holding on doggedly to their faith, living in what one person described as a spirit of 'constructive criticism and co-operation' with the state. Some of the young people spoke particularly about the frustration they felt at the restrictions that prevented them from travelling beyond East Germany. I recorded an interview with one theological student whose English was excellent. When I asked him where he had learned to speak with such a flawless accent, he said, 'Through listening to the BBC World Service!' We were invited to meet the President of the Republic, Erich Honecker, and were able to raise questions with him about the need for young people to be enabled to have wider ecumenical contacts. We felt the stirrings of closer relations beginning between East and West Germany.

It was in West Berlin that the Central Committee was held in the summer of 1974. Immediately preceding it was another landmark WCC meeting – the Conference on 'Sexism in the '70s'. The title provoked some ribaldry. For many people 'Sexism' was a new word in their vocabulary. Those of us planning the consultation chose it deliberately because of its analogy with 'racism'. We regarded discrimination on grounds of gender as sinful and indeed as heretical as discrimination on grounds of race, since both deny a dignity that is God-given. I personally had been much influenced by the feminist movement which found strong expression in Betty Friedan's book, published in America while I was there in 1964, and entitled *The Feminine Mystique*. Like many ground-breaking books, it had been subjected to ridicule and to misrepresentation but it became one of those books that raised the awareness of a whole generation of women across the world.

Gender discrimination was no new subject for the WCC to tackle. One of the major addresses at the Amsterdam Assembly had been on *The Service and Status of Women in the Church*, given by the distinguished Anglican educationalist Kathleen Bliss. It was based on the findings of a world-wide study into the work of women in all the major denominations joining the WCC. As a result of this study a permanent commission was set up in the WCC, later to become known as the Department of Co-operation of Men and Women in Church, Family and Society. For 20 years it was led by the indomitable Madeleine Barot. Brigalia Bam, who was living in Geneva in exile from South Africa, had four years before taken over the leadership from Madeleine's immediate successor, Rena Karefa Smart of Sierra Leone.

Brigalia and I together chaired the Sexism Consultation, which brought together 160 women from 49 countries. It was a prophetic gathering, in the sense that, as the prophets used to say, the word of God '*happened*' among us. It was more of an event than just a meeting. As two of the posters adorning the walls expressed it, 'Sisterhood is blooming – Springtime will never be the same again'. I think many of us found it a surprisingly liberating experience to be at a women-only conference! The only man invited to address the consultation was Philip Potter, who, as a Caribbean man, paid a tribute to what he called 'the grace, grit and gumption of women' who had often in his part of the world borne the heaviest burdens of slavery and its aftermath.

The most important impact of the consultation came through the intense group discussions and the many recommendations that emerged from them, to be passed on to the central bodies of the WCC and to be taken back by the participants to the member churches. This was but the beginning of a process leading to a world-wide study on the 'Community of Women and Men in the Church' which provoked a still continuing debate, reaching a climax at an international consultation held in Sheffield in 1981 and leading eventually to a Decade of the Churches in Solidarity with Women which was launched in 1988.

As we went straight on from the Sexism Consultation into the Central Committee held in the Congress Hall in West Berlin, I was able to report on it there with immediate enthusiasm. It was agreed that a whole session of the next Assembly should be handed over to women as a time for sharing their concerns about the role of women in church and society. The rest of the Central Committee was fully occupied in preparations for that Assembly. At this last moment we had been advised that it would not be safe or wise for a major Christian gathering to be held in Djakarta, in the light of there being considerable unrest there. Indonesian church leaders were disappointed, but African churches rose to the occasion and welcomed the opportunity to invite us to meet in Nairobi in the summer of 1975.

In view of the theme 'Jesus Christ Frees and Unites' the Fifth Assembly was planned to be as informal and festive as possible. The delegates from the 271 member churches from all parts of the world were invited to gather in the forecourt of the Jomo Kenyatta Conference Centre, without any particular protocol, and dressed where appropriate in national costume. Nevertheless, somehow amid the milling throng a procession managed to assemble itself, led by the Orthodox in their ecclesiastical robes! Torrential rain drove us indoors, but not before we had heard the ringing tones of the Archbishop of Kenya opening the gathering with the announcement, 'The Lord, even the most mighty God, hath spoken and called the world!' He was immediately interrupted by an intruder, who by this time was well known to me as a familiar heckler, the Scotsman Jack Glass, from the so-called Twentieth Century Reformation Movement. Kenyan police rapidly removed him and his two colleagues and later we had to go and plead for them to be released from gaol! Meanwhile the opening service proceeded in the Hall with a young Masai girl carrying in the Bible, which was to be a focus of our study throughout the week.

A presentation of the main theme through a study of the biblical parable of the Prodigal Son was particularly memorable. It was led by two Donalds – Donald Coggan, the Archbishop of Canterbury, accompanied by the popular British revue artist Donald Swann. They invited us to imagine the story as it might work out in our various cultures today. (The Americans for example suggested that there it might just as likely be a prodigal daughter, while Africans envisaged the whole extended family being concerned about the boy's recklessness.) A powerful theological exposition of the theme came from an American Presbyterian theologian, Dr McAfee Brown, who posed the question Jesus asked at Caesarea Philippi, 'Who do you say that I am?' He spoke of Jesus as Liberator, Divider and Unifier. The African churches presented a powerful drama written by Joe de Graft, a Ghanaian studying at the University of Nairobi, following Africa's journey from an age of innocence into a time of exploration and exploitation and then of the struggle for independence, with all the present-day follies and tyrannies. It was an honest, haunting and at times lyrical presentation.

Professor Charles Birch of Sydney University, speaking on

'Creation, Technology and Human Development' reminded us that in Kenya we were near what might be thought of as the cradle of human life. He went on to warn us that we could be heading, like the *Titanic*, towards its destruction. He spoke of the five 'icebergs' looming ahead – overpopulation, scarcity of food, shortage of fossil fuels, environmental deterioration and war. This prophetic warning ended with the biblical exhortation to 'replenish the earth'. The resulting discussion in Section VI of the Assembly, concerned with human development and the ambiguities of power and technology, led to a new major programme emphasis in the WCC on The Search for a Just, Participatory and Sustainable Society. Despite the clumsy title, its challenge to Christians to live more responsibly, not only in relation to their fellow human beings but in reverence for the whole of creation, has become increasingly relevant as we have become more aware of the current threat of climate change and of environmental damage.

Another major concern of this Assembly was the search for the unity not only of the Church but of the whole of humanity. The constant refrain of the Assembly became the words of one of the prayers, set to music by a young German pop music group who frequently had us all singing and dancing, 'Break down the walls that separate us and unite us in a single body'.

In a powerful plenary session called 'That they all may be one', led by Mercy Oduyoye of Nigeria, there were testimonies and confessions from many parts of the world demonstrating that the question of unity was no mere academic issue, but in some places literally a matter of life and death. 'We have learned in Northern Ireland', came the agonized cry of Gordon Grey, 'that divided churches can eventually cost lives.' 'How can the church maintain unity among members fighting one another on the battlefield?' cried Manas Buthelezi from South Africa. 'The gospel is betrayed', declared Wesley Ariarajah from Sri Lanka, 'when, in a country divided by caste, language, culture and creed, it fails to express the oneness that Christ brings.' Following the discussion on unity, the churches were asked to respond to the agreed statements on Baptism, Eucharist and Ministry compiled by the commission on Faith and Order.

The special session requested by the women was duly held. Women from Australia, from the Near East Council of Churches and from Kenya spoke of their personal experiences as women working in the 'man's world' of the church or of politics. In a following panel discussion Justice Annie Jiagge of Ghana, Ms Prakai Nontawassee, a theologian from Thailand and Dr Una Kroll from the United Kingdom went into deeper analysis of the reasons for sexist discrimination. It was excellent material but unfortunately overran the allocated time by more than an hour. One woman commented, 'We've been kept silent so long. What do they expect when we are at last given a chance to speak?'

For MM and me the responsibility of chairing such a lively Assembly had its tense moments. Particularly protracted and complicated was the debate on public affairs, when the recently signed agreement on disarmament made between the Soviet-bloc countries and western European states, known as the Helsinki Agreement, came under discussion. References in the Helsinki Agreement to religious liberty prompted several resolutions from those wanting to point particularly to the restrictions placed on religious liberty and on human rights in the USSR. All such resolutions were strenuously resisted by the Russian delegation. Numerous amendments and counter-amendments followed. Eventually a statement generally commending the text of the Helsinki Agreement but adding a section recognizing the different conditions and political systems under which churches were working in various parts of the world was agreed by a large majority, the Russian Orthodox delegation abstaining from the vote.[3]

The special hearing devoted to this issue meant that there was a large company of people in the plenary hall when the time came to close business for the day. On the spur of the moment I sent a scribbled note down to Metropolitan Nikodim asking if he would lead our closing prayers. He came up to the platform accompanied by his fellow Russian delegates. Together they formed a choir and led us in a liturgy of evening prayer that was timeless and deeply moving. It was one of those moments when, in spite of all political pressures, worship really did break down the walls between us.

---

3 The full text of the resolution and of the Russian statement explaining the abstention from voting can be read in '*Breaking Barriers*' Report of the Nairobi Assembly, ed. David Paton, SPCK, 1975, pp. 172–4.

# 8

# *New Partnerships*

❧

As 1975 was International Women's Year, I was involved with Betty Hares, my colleague in the Methodist Overseas Division, in planning a spectacular programme in the Royal Albert Hall. We entitled it 'Signs of Hope – a Celebration of Good News for Men and Women in Today's World.' The presentation included choral and instrumental music, solos and ballet, displays of gymnastics and of fashion. The main speaker was Gwen Konie, a young Zambian woman diplomat. Following her address was a lively panel discussion between four distinguished women: Mrs Kantra Dogra, an Indian political scientist; Dr Una Kroll, a deaconess and doctor in Southwark; Ms Sadie Patterson, an active Trade Unionist and leader of *Women Together,* a bridge-building movement in Northern Ireland; and Mrs Adelaide Tambo of the African National Congress Women's League of South Africa.

We included in the programme a message I had brought from the Executive Committee of the World Council of Churches:

As Christians we affirm that the equality of women and men is clearly enunciated in the gospel of Jesus Christ and we rejoice in all that has been done in the name of that gospel to minister to the spiritual, mental and physical needs of women in all six continents – we look forward eagerly towards the day when women and men together can work for a world community, in which all are free to utilize their God-given talents in the service of a new humanity.

The event was not without its critics. Adelaide Tambo's presence drew the protests of those who wanted to deny any voice to the African National Congress, banned in South Africa. There were others who were offended by Una Kroll's ardent campaign for the ordination of women in the Anglican Church. Nevertheless, the Albert Hall was crowded to its capacity by an audience, mainly of women, who had travelled from all over the country – a sign of hope in itself.

This celebration was a recognition of the fact that we were becoming such a mixed society in Britain that we could draw on the talents of people of many nations and cultures. Inspired by a visionary layman, Brian Frost, we had embarked at this time on many ventures which celebrated the diversity to be found in London. In particular, in a week-long Festival of the Spirit, we explored different traditions of spirituality that could be experienced within the close vicinity of the city. That festival reached its climax in a glorious, open-air celebration of the Eucharist in Trafalgar Square on the Sunday of Pentecost 1973. It was a truly ecumenical occasion, with a choir of Pentecostalists, a procession of clergy of all denominations, myself a lay preacher, and Bishop Colin Winter, Anglican bishop in exile from Namibia, in full liturgical vestments, acting as the celebrant. In the square was gathered a crowd like that on the first Pentecost 'from every nation under heaven'. All were invited to take of the bread and the wine and most of the crowd did, including, to the horror of some traditionalists, even an occasional pigeon who gobbled up the crumbs on the paving stones! So great was the jubilation that when the service was over, dancing spontaneously broke out all round the square, a scene happily captured by a photograph that made the front page of the *Guardian* the next day.

My new responsibilities at the Overseas Division meant that I was soon away on my travels again. But things had changed a lot since the leisurely journeys I once enjoyed by sea. Now it was a matter of just a few hours' flight and a month allowed for an official visit to Nigeria, Ghana and Sierra Leone with the primary purpose of liaison with the presiding officers of these now largely autonomous churches. In no way was a visit from an 'Area Secretary' regarded any longer as 'oversight'. For me it was more a journey of orientation where my role was that of a diplomat discussing policy or of a partner responding to requests for aid in the form either of finance or personnel. My itinerary was entirely in the hands of the church leaders and they chose to take me to see such projects as they wanted to commend for increased support from the church in Britain. In days when correspondence was still slow and phone calls were expensive, such person-to-person contact was of paramount importance and I was grateful for the opportunity of making it.

So, in Nigeria, accompanied by the conference accountant, a photographer and the press officer, I was taken on a ceremonial visit to the huge central church in Tinubu Square, Lagos and then up country to Abeokuta, where my father had served over 50 years before as a missionary. To my astonishment there were people there who still vividly remembered him, though they must have been small children at the time. One old man could even quote things he had said in his sermons. It would seem that one advantage of cultures which are still primarily oral is that memory for the spoken word remains extraordinarily clear. Although I was not born until long after my parents returned to England, the people in Abeokuta insisted on calling me 'Obomawale' – child come home.

My discussions with the Conference officers centred most on

how the church in the different areas of Nigeria was seeking ways of reconciliation after the rift of the war with Biafra and what hope there was of any progress towards unity within the Nigerian nation as well as in the Church. The nation's boundaries had been arbitrarily drawn by the colonialists. There was no common history as one people but rather a difficult coalescence of vastly different tribes with their own distinctive languages and cultures.

A few hours' flight took me from Lagos to Accra, where I was the guest of the President of the Methodist Conference and invited to preach in the Methodist church in Cape Coast. The pulpit there is built over the grave of the first three missionaries to arrive in what was then known as 'the white man's grave', none of whom had survived more than a few months. It was when the preacher Thomas Birch Freeman, himself of African descent, answered the call to come from Britain that the Christian gospel began to take root in Ghanaian soil. On such honoured sacrifice was the present, strong church in Ghana built, a church markedly still faithful to the Wesleyan tradition in both liturgy and theology, which many of its people are now bringing back to the church in Britain.

Ghana is a much more compact country than Nigeria and had not suffered the trauma of civil war. During an extensive tour up to Wa in the northern territories I was impressed by the close cooperation I saw between Methodists and their Roman Catholic colleagues, some of whom were 'white fathers' from the missionary community in North London. Further south we went on a long journey by motor boat and then canoe to what seemed a sparsely inhabited area until we arrived at a river bank where a great reception was awaiting us. The local chief was seated under a large, golden umbrella surrounded by drummers and dancers welcoming us as honoured visitors. Beside the chief was a carved, curved stool on which I was invited to sit, to signify that I had come as a friend. The stool was then presented to me as a gift and the chief expressed the hope that that area would be regarded as a priority in the church's planning for the extension of medical work into those remote villages. The Ghanaian church was clearly eager to move forward in mission.

My first view of the 'Sitting Lion' mountain that gives Sierra Leone its name was on the spectacular journey by ferry-boat along the peninsula from the airport. The crowded city of Freetown reminded me of the Caribbean with its mixed population, many of whom were descendants of freed slaves. Their language is a fascinating Creole, a mixture of English, with French and odd Yoruba or Fante words included. Up country the land, the Mende people and the language are very different.

Sierra Leone was years later to erupt in a horrendous outbreak of widespread violence. The worst crimes we encountered while I was there were those in the area of Koidu, centre of the diamond trade, such an easy commodity to steal and to smuggle. We even heard of one gang of thieves tunnelling their way under the police station itself! It was the illicit trade in such gems that helped to fuel the ensuing tribal warfare.

At a formal reception in the main Methodist church in Freetown I was presented with a gift from my African hosts – a gloriously embroidered robe, specially made to my own measurements! I never cease to marvel at the gracious generosity which is typical of African hospitality. Later, when we heard news of fighting throughout the country, we wept with the church throughout Sierra Leone, particularly as it witnessed the devastation of such splendid institutions as the Segbwema hospital and the many primary and secondary schools built up through the past century and now needing to be rebuilt. It was only after a decade of particularly brutal atrocities that peace was finally restored to the country under a UN peace-keeping operation aided by British troops.

My main area of responsibility as an Area officer at this time was one of liaison with the Conference of the Methodist Church in the Caribbean and Americas, which had become autonomous in 1967. The very name of the Conference indicates something of the complexity faced by those seeking to weld together in one Conference a mosaic of churches in islands scattered over an ocean covering an area more extensive than the whole of Western Europe, from Scandinavia to Sicily, with an even greater variety of cultures and languages.

The headquarters of the new Conference was situated in the island of Antigua, which might well be regarded as the cradle of world Methodism. On this island the historic meeting took place on Christmas day 1786 between Thomas Coke, John Wesley's emissary to America, escaping from a shipwreck, and John Baxter, a Methodist lay preacher who had been working in Nelson's dockyard. For some years Baxter had been preaching to a large congregation of slaves, who had remained faithful to the gospel ever since three of their number had accompanied their owner, Nathaniel Gilbert, to London in 1760. There these women as well as Gilbert himself heard John Wesley preach and had asked for baptism. Back home in Antigua they had gathered a great congregation of fellow slaves together and from the steps of Nathaniel Gilbert's house had shared their liberating experience and their new-found joy in the gospel. For over 20 years the slaves continued to pray that preachers might come from Britain to minister to them, and at about 5 am on that historic Christmas Day, 1786, Thomas Coke himself arrived, driven to seek shelter from the storm at sea, at an hour that has been commemorated in Antigua on every Christmas Day since.

On my first secretarial tour of the Caribbean in 1973, I was made aware of the extraordinary history of the peoples of this region. The original inhabitants of islands like Dominica had been Caribs, an indomitable race of people who had fled into the mountains to escape the attacks of invading colonists from various parts of Europe. Then came the effects of what John Wesley in his letter to William Wilberforce called that 'execrable villainy', the slave trade. Through it hordes of people of a variety of African tribes were shipped to the islands, deprived of their family names, separated from their language groups and forced to work on the sugar plantations owned by European settlers. Their survival of this shameful period in human history has given the people of the Caribbean an amazing resilience and a reliance on more than mere human strength which finds expression in the deep spirituality of their music and in the continuing strength of their religious faith.

In one sense my first visit to the area was a visit back into history, but in another way it was one of those experiences when 'coming events cast their shadow before'. I went there just at the time when I personally was moving house, having bought a flat in my own birthplace, Wembley. I had joined the Methodist church in Harlesden, where already by then the majority of the congregation were people who had come from the Caribbean to live in the borough of Brent. I found it helpful to share at first hand the traditions that had grown up in Caribbean Methodism, in many ways closer to the Wesleyan traditions introduced by nineteenth-century missionaries than to the post-war radical developments in worship and theology that had become widespread in Britain. I also came to appreciate something of the shock it must have been to many of those immigrants when at first they were hardly recognized by fellow Methodists in Britain.

In the lovely island of Antigua itself, I was able to visit the historic sites – the homes of Lord Nelson, of John Baxter and of Nathaniel Gilbert, the plantation owner on whose estate the Methodist work began. We discussed plans for the renovating of Gilbert's house to turn it into some kind of ecumenical, residential centre. I was invited to preach in the little chapel known as the

Gilbert Memorial, where I was glad to see commemorated in a plaque on the wall the names of Bessie, Sophia and Mary Alleyne, the women who accompanied Nathaniel Gilbert to London and who responded there to John Wesley's preaching and were baptized by him.

I was also invited to preach in the large central church in St John's known as Ebenezer. I noted in my journal how impressed I was by a young teenage organist there who played the hymns with great gusto and kept us all spellbound at the end as we listened to his spirited postlude, 'Glory, glory, hallelujah!' I didn't note it at the time, but the boy's name was Robert Maginley, who fifteen years later responded to a call to serve in the ministry in Britain. As he prepared his candidature, he came under my tuition at Harlesden and I have regarded him as a dear 'son in the gospel' ever since.

Many of the discussions I had during my secretarial visit to the Caribbean area concerned the role of missionaries in a church that wanted to be free of any paternalism from the church in Britain and was developing new kinds of partnerships. In the past, many missionaries had given a life-time of service in the Caribbean and had left their distinctive influence on the church there. Particularly noticeable for example was the strength of the Wesley Deaconess Order, inspired by the leadership of Sister Jessie Kerridge, who had tirelessly visited all the islands encouraging young women in a sense of vocation. I was impressed too by the number of prestigious church secondary schools I saw in the Caribbean, all with strict codes of discipline and smart uniforms, modelled on British 'public' schools, following a British syllabus and still depending to some extent on expatriate help. In Queens College in the Bahamas, for instance, where there were over 1,800 students, almost all the teachers were British.

In Haiti, the poorest of the islands, many projects among the poorest of the poor were church-initiated and relied heavily on the help of skilled professionals who came from the United States or Canada to give short-term voluntary service. Haiti was proud of having been historically the first island to resist occupation by foreigners, yet ironically it seemed to be now the most dependent of the islands on foreign aid. The church was finding it increasingly difficult to maintain the Methodist circuit system, there being a dearth of candidates for the ministry and hardly any local lay leadership. The missionaries who were still serving there were questioning their role as a kind of 'stop-gap ministry'. The urgent need, I was told, was for local leaders trained in methods of community development for the many projects in a land of such political and economic turmoil.

The consensus I found among the West Indian ministers throughout the Caribbean was that they welcomed as colleagues people from overseas and the richer, international experience brought by them, but they wanted such partnership to take the form of short-term rather than long-term periods of service and to be subject to the stationing requirements of the Caribbean Conference itself.

Hearing and seeing so much of the vitality of the church in the Caribbean, and particularly appreciating the eloquence of so much of the preaching I heard there, I ventured to suggest that what we needed now was a mission *to* Britain rather than one *from* Britain. We invited the Methodist Church of the Caribbean to send a mission team to work in north-west London for a month, both in a pastoral visit to Caribbean people now settling in Britain but also in an evangelical enterprise stirring the church in Britain into a new awareness of the demands of the gospel and the multiracial nature of the Church. The response was generous. The President of the Caribbean Conference himself, the Revd Claude Cadogan, led an excellent team which included a promising probationer minister, the Revd George Mulrain (now, incidentally, himself the President of the Caribbean Conference), a young deaconess, Sonia James, and a lay member of the church in the Bahamas, Marie Murray. In response to that mission we were able to undertake the training of more West Indians as local preachers and class leaders in the churches in north-west London. In Harlesden we began an Opportunity for Ministry programme to encourage more young black men and women living in Britain to offer for the ministry.

As an expression of the closer relationship growing in Britain between the Anglican and Methodist Churches, plans had been made for a joint mission to be launched in Argentina, to be known as AMPLA – Anglican Methodist Project in Latin America. To explore the possibilities of such a partnership, I was sent on a six-week journey across South and Central America, and also up into the Caribbean area again, visiting in all over 20 different nations in a kind of whistle-stop tour. In most of the countries I visited in Latin America the Methodist churches were more closely related to the Board of Global Missions in New York than to British Methodism. I encountered en route some bewilderment about the new Anglican–Methodist project, which, some felt, was an initiative coming from the 'top level' of the two churches in Britain rather than from consultation with people on the ground. It seemed to me that this is frequently one of the perils of ecumenical plans. If ecumenism is only imposed from above and does not spring up from the grassroots, it will not grow.

I was given a warm welcome on arrival in Buenos Aires, where I was met by the ardent feminist and Argentinian scholar and theologian, Beatriz Couch. She took me straight to ISEDET, the Higher Evangelical Institute of Theological Studies, where, together with visitors from a theological college in Brazil, we were entertained to an enormous barbecue with so many varieties of meat being served that I lost count of how many courses we had. People were immediately eager to question me about the WCC. I was told that it was regarded by the government in Argentina as a subversive organization, a fact which, I gathered, enhanced its reputation among the theological students and staff! Certainly I was soon made aware of how repressive was the military regime which had now seized power in Argentina. Already many people known to be opponents of the junta were 'disappearing', and the weekly ritual had begun of women gathering in the Plaza de Mayo in the city centre every Thursday to stand in silent protest and prayer for their missing relatives.

Beatriz took me by a short plane journey across the River Plate, the widest river in the world, to Uruguay. We met the President of the Methodist Church there who, for safety's sake, operated from two addresses, one in Montevideo as head of the church and the other in Buenos Aires as a worker for human rights. One young minister I met had himself recently suffered imprisonment and even torture for his protests against violations of human rights. He described to me the dilemma he still felt in being a preacher of the gospel with a prophetic ministry to fulfil, and yet knowing that his message could in fact result in his being given another prison sentence – 'and these are no ordinary prisons', he said, 'they can totally destroy a person'.

I asked what help from the Church in Britain would be the most effective in this situation. Both here and in other parts of Latin America I was told repeatedly that the Church there welcomed every contact with other parts of the world-wide Church. It gave a kind of protection to those under threat in their own lands when it was known that they had international support and visibility.

The flight over the Andes mountains up the long narrow extent of Chile was breathtaking in the gigantic grandeur of the snow-capped mountain peaks. But on the ground the sense of the looming presence of the military dictatorship of Pinochet was all-pervasive. Wandering alone through the city of Santiago I went into the massive, baroque cathedral and noticed next door to it the offices of the *Vicaria de la Solidaridad.* There I was shown a moving exhibition of handicrafts – collages made up of scraps of material, illustrating scenes in the lives of some of the poorer people of the city, and a beautiful series of representations of the Stations of the Cross, placing these events in the context of the contemporary suffering of the people of Chile with whom so many courageous people in both the Catholic and the Protestant Churches were expressing total solidarity.

Landing a few days later in La Paz was rather like landing on the moon. The airport is the highest in the world and the landscape lunar in appearance. A slip-up in arrangements meant there was no-one to meet me so, going down the mountainside in a rickety taxi, I quickly fell prey to the mountain sickness of which I should have been wary at such a high altitude. But, as I've discovered often when travelling, there is always kindness at hand and despite the fact that the hotels were full, someone found a bed for me and managed to contact the local Methodist minister. He came immediately to fetch me to his home next door to a large, prestigious college, an American Methodist foundation.

Over a cup of tea we had an interesting discussion about the liberation theology which had developed out of the Latin American situation during the 1960s. 'What we need now', he said, 'is a theology of captivity. Our situation is no longer revolutionary; it is repressive. The Church's role now is to give people hope and to witness to the dignity of human beings and to the sovereignty of God in a society where both seem to be denied.' He drew his inspiration from the prophets of the captivity like Jeremiah and from the end vision of the book of Revelation.

The ecumenical projects I was taken to see in Bolivia were indeed future-oriented – one a tree-planting project in the *alto plano*, the high plain up in the mountains where there are large areas of flat scrubland with just a few scattered farmsteads. The roots of the trees were intended to help stabilize the soil and so prevent the dangers of soil erosion, while the branches would provide shelter from the fierce winds. Thus attempts were being made to change the whole ecology of the area; I reflected that ecology and ecumenism are closely linked, both being concerned with the welfare of the one world.

The next stage of my journey gave me a tantalizing overnight stop in Lima, where I had time to admire the elegance of the Spanish plazas in the centre of town and gaze aghast at the poverty of the shanty towns on the outskirts. I travelled on up into the Caribbean area via Caracas and Curaçao to Georgetown in Guyana, where the inaugural conference of the Caribbean Council of Churches was being held. A unique feature of this Council was that from the first day the Roman Catholic Church was included in full membership and Archbishop Pantin of Trinidad was prominent in the leadership. The Prime Minister of Guyana, Forbes Burnham, gave a speech of welcome. This was followed by a trenchant analysis of the human rights situation in many parts of the Caribbean given in a powerful speech by Philip Potter, a prophet who in this instance was by no means without honour in his own country. Following that we were treated to a dazzling display of Guyanese culture presented by the National Dance Theatre. The other most memorable feature of the Council meeting for me was that a selection of new hymns had been written specially for it, one of which – 'The right hand of God' – has since gained world-wide popularity.

The remainder of my marathon journey took me to areas of the Caribbean and of Central America which I had visited before as Area Secretary. There I was mainly concerned with personnel matters, as more missionaries were coming to the end of their term of service and it seemed unlikely that they would be replaced. There were also some complicated legal issues concerning church properties owned under various jurisdictions in the different islands and yet all now being transferred from the Methodist Missionary Society to the autonomous Conference with its headquarters in Antigua. Meanwhile I had opportunities to renew old friendships with people throughout the Caribbean, some of whom had returned there after time spent in Britain, or were related to people living there now, and others who had welcomed me so warmly on past occasions when I had visited their churches.

Back home in Britain I had now been asked to chair the British Council of Churches' Community and Race Relations Unit. It was during the time when Idi Amin was driving Ugandan Asians out of his country. The staff of CRRU gave energy and resources in trying to help them settle here and on educating the British public to receive them.

I look back with shamed humility on that time, when a group of us on the WCC Executive Committee asked one of our members, Janani Luwum, the newly elected Archbishop of Uganda, why the Church was not protesting against Idi Amin. With his gentle smile, he quietly replied, 'We shall know when the right time comes and God wants us to speak out'. A few months later, we heard that the Archbishop had written a letter of quiet but prophetic rebuke to his ruler. Within hours he was arrested. An eyewitness described how, still dressed in his purple cassock, the archbishop was hauled before a crowd of soldiers shouting for his blood. He was silent, except for the sad shaking of his head in response to the accusations that were made against him. They led him away and he was killed. Later when we were meeting in the Executive Committee a cable came from his Church announcing the news 'The archbishop has gone home to his Lord'. The following Sunday, we were told, a massive crowd gathered at the cathedral for his funeral. They had prepared the grave and only at the last minute were told that they could not have the body. The mourners wept bitterly until one woman exclaimed, 'The grave is empty! But the Lord is risen!'

I was soon to need that kind of faith myself when once again I had to face the emptiness and silence of bereavement. My sister Muriel who had been a skilled nurse herself had now for several months been fighting her own battle against breast cancer. We spent a precious holiday together in which I tried to share her pain with her and she shared her faith with me. She faced death unafraid, but my other sister, Joy, and I now felt very bereft, the only ones left of what had been such a close-knit family.

In 1976 the British Council of Churches had published a hard hitting pamphlet by Gus John entitled *The New Black Presence in Britain*, reminding readers of the history of the treatment of black people in this country. In an admirable Foreword Bishop David Sheppard wrote: 'I go along with the view that black people have not brought problems to Britain, but have revealed the problems our society already had.'[1]

In reaction to the increasing activity of the National Front we formed an organization called Christians Against Racism and Fascism. In a large rally in Hyde Park we staged a symbolic cleansing of the Union Jack, reclaiming it as the flag of a multiracial society capable of embracing a diversity of cultures. Fortunately the weather was good and we were supported by celebrities from the entertainments world – Nadia Cattouse the folk singer and Ian Hall the organist and choir director.

Meanwhile members of the National Front continued to spread their racist propaganda. As the General Election of 1979 approached they managed to persuade the Ealing Council to permit them to hold an election meeting in the Town Hall in

---

1 Gus John, *The New Black Presence in Britain: a Christian Scrunity*, BCC, 1976, foreword.

Southall. Anyone who knows Southall would know that by 1979 there were not likely to be members of the National Front living in that largely Asian constituency! In a petition signed by over 19,000 residents the local population protested against the meeting. Many literally sat down in front of the Town Hall to prevent its being held. The police were ordered to break up the protest and a mêlée resulted in which hundreds of young Asians were arrested and one young New Zealander trying to get away from the scene was bashed on the head and died from his injuries. His name was Blair Peach and his death signalled how dangerous the struggle against racism was becoming in Britain.

There were demands for an official enquiry into the circumstances of Blair Peach's death. When these were refused, Patricia Hewitt, who was at that time Director of the Council for Civil Liberties, convened a team to undertake an unofficial enquiry under the chairmanship of Michael Dummett, the Wykeham Professor of Logic at Oxford University. Under his leadership those of us on the enquiry panel spent many hours in Southall interviewing eyewitnesses of the event and coming to the conclusion that there was no doubt that Blair Peach had been the innocent victim of injuries inflicted by police truncheons. Pat Hewitt, accompanied by Michael Dummett, Joan Lestor MP, the Bishop of Willesden and myself, took our report to the Home Secretary, William Whitelaw. He gave us a sympathetic hearing but refused to order any further enquiry. A couple of years later, after riots in Brixton, he did appoint Lord Scarman to chair a full enquiry into that situation and as one result the Police Complaints Commission was set up. So, little by little, it seemed that Britain was beginning to learn that strenuous efforts were needed to ensure the protection and promotion of racial justice in this country as well as world-wide.

I was not sorry when the Central Committee of the World

Council of Churches chose to hold its 1979 meeting in Jamaica. Although I was no longer an officer of the Central Committee I had been appointed at the Nairobi Assembly to continue as a member of the Executive and I was still deeply involved in the Commission of the by now notorious Programme to Combat Racism. The situation in South Africa had deteriorated. In 1976 over 10,000 school children in Soweto had taken to the streets in protest against laws affecting their education, and the police had fired on them, killing at least 300. This had shocked the world into realizing the extent of the violence of the apartheid regime. The announcement in autumn 1978 of grants from the Special Fund of the PCR being given to the Patriotic Front, which was by then engaged in armed struggle against the illegal regime in Rhodesia, had caused an even greater furore than the first announcement in 1970 of grants given to the ANC in South Africa.

In the Central Committee we faced fierce criticism of the whole PCR programme from members representing churches in Ireland and in Germany, but there was an equally spirited defence of it from African Church leaders and from Archbishop Ted Scott of Canada, who was by then the Chairman of the Central Committee. He personally had been subjected to vitriolic attacks in the Canadian press when the Special Fund grants were announced but he had subsequently won the support and confidence of the Canadian churches. Eventually he was nominated as Canada's representative on the Commonwealth's 'Eminent Persons Group' set up to try to resolve the apartheid crisis in South Africa and the concurrent divisions within the Commonwealth.

Jamaica itself was caught up in violence while we were meeting there, as roads were blockaded off to protect the city from rioters protesting against the increase in oil prices. Michael Manley, the Prime Minister, nevertheless gave an up-beat address to the Central Committee emphasizing the necessity for a new international economic order if nations like Jamaica were ever to be relieved of the burdens imposed upon them by their dependence upon financial borrowing and foreign investment.

Throughout our stay in the fine campus of the University of the West Indies we were given armed guards and warned to be particularly security conscious whenever we went beyond the campus grounds. But that still didn't prevent us from enjoying a relaxing day trip to the splendid beaches of Ocho Rios, where the sight of prelates of all shapes and sizes doffing their ecclesiastical vestments and donning bathing suits was a welcome exercise in ecumenical egalitarianism! As one onlooker remarked, 'You couldn't tell a bishop from a layman', to which came the wicked reply, 'The bishops are usually the ones swimming against the tide!'

A small group of us took the opportunity of going on from Jamaica for a short visit to Cuba. We arrived in Havana at the same time as a large jet from Miami, bringing a host of returning Cuban exiles for a brief visit back home. The difference between their sophisticated appearance and the simpler dress of the locals welcoming them indicated straightaway the difference in life style between the two societies. After 20 years of socialist revolution Cubans seemed to have learned a discipline which had changed their sense of values. Yet it was disturbing to see how the crowds clamoured around the tourist shops, where returning Americans poured out their dollars in plying Cuban relatives with luxuries they had learned to live without.

Discipline seemed to be characteristic of Cuban society. We noted how workmen on construction sites of new blocks of flats were given an incentive to work well by the promise that they would be able to choose and live in one of the flats themselves! Women who came to work in large firms were given the option of leaving their children in the child-care facilities provided by the firm but only on condition that parents attended classes in parenting skills and worked in co-operation with the carers. The specialist schools we saw reminded us of hot-houses where children with any particular gifts were given a rigorous education, but still expected to do work on the land. All young professionally qualified people had to give a period of voluntary service in the community. It was impressive to meet squads of young doctors and nurses training for a period of service in local rural areas or overseas in Africa. We noted that there was not only a minimum wage but a maximum one too.

The churches, which before the revolution had large missionary staffs and generous financial support mainly from the USA, had by force of circumstance become independent of any outside help. With a small local ministry they still maintained a strong witness. In the church where I was invited to preach there was a congregation of over 100, many of them young people. Despite the discipline the exuberant Caribbean creativity kept breaking through. The church leaders we met particularly welcomed the new 'open door' policy of the Cuban government which had made it possible for us to visit and for them to share in ecumenical events such as the new Caribbean Conference of Churches. They joined us in singing the CCC hymn 'The right hand of God is writing in our land', but wittily suggested that perhaps we should affirm that the left hand of God was working there too!

I had by this time almost reached the end of my six-year term of office as Area Secretary for the Caribbean. I returned home, wrote and submitted my various reports, and wondered where the next chapter in my life would take me.

# 9

## A Voice in the World

Wherever I travelled there was one tune which, like a lullaby, comforted me with thoughts of home. It was *Lillibullero*, the signature tune of the BBC World Service. Almost everywhere I went I had good reception on my short wave radio so I became a life-long addict of the World Service. When in London I was a frequent visitor to Bush House, headquarters of the External Services, an imposing building standing in the middle of Aldwych. It was originally built in the 1920s as an American Trade Centre by a Mr Irving T. Bush of the Bush Terminal Company of New York. Although it had housed a few radio studios, more were added when the BBC European Services moved there after bombs had damaged Broadcasting House in 1941. Building works seemed to have been going on there ever since, in attempts to adapt the premises to the growing needs of what became known as the BBC External Services. That included all the foreign language services as well as the output in English specifically known as 'World Service'. (After 1988 the whole operation was called the BBC World Service.)

I was often invited to the studios to take part in World Service discussions about the World Council of Churches and its controversial Programme to Combat Racism, which seemed to be constantly in the news, or to be interviewed by some of the language services about my various journeys in areas to which they were particularly broadcasting.

At that time the Organiser of Religious Broadcasting Overseas, known according to BBC custom by the impressive acronym ORBO, was an Anglican priest, the Revd Colin Semper. He invited me to work with him on some 'pilots' for a series of religious discussion programmes he was planning, to be concerned with ethical dilemmas. I became fascinated by the whole process of radio production. Colin told me that he was soon moving over to Broadcasting House, to what was known in the External Services as the 'domestic' part of the BBC's output. He had been appointed as Head of Religious Radio and would be working as a close colleague of a former colleague of mine, the Revd Colin Morris, who had recently become Head of Religious Television. To my astonishment, the two Colins between them suggested to me that I should apply for the post of ORBO.

Though I had done plenty of broadcasting and script-writing I had no experience of radio production and I was by this time 50 years of age. Most people I knew on the staff of the BBC had been there since they graduated, and in religious broadcasting many senior producers in those days were ordained clerics. So I didn't think there was much point in my applying for the post. I went to talk with a wise spiritual adviser, Canon Trevor Beeson of Westminster Abbey, who encouraged me to think through all the possible options for the next decade of my working life and to consider prayerfully which would make the fullest use of the world-wide experience I had been privileged to enjoy. So I was emboldened to reply to the BBC advertisement and to face what is known in BBC circles as a 'board', a formidable interviewing panel on which I met Austen Kark, the genial but perceptive Managing Director of the External Services. He plied me with searching questions about how I would deal with the many controversial issues that arose constantly in religious affairs and what I understood by the term 'neutrality', one of the principles of BBC broadcasting.

No-one was more astonished nor more delighted than I was when I was actually appointed to the post, to begin in September 1979. There was a lot of comment in the press at the time that I was not only the first lay person and non-Anglican to become ORBO, but that I was one of the first women to be given a senior post in religious broadcasting. I could only think that it was my address book that had proved to be my best qualification. Over the years I had been on personal speaking terms with the heads of most of the major churches across the world, and so I possessed that most valuable commodity for broadcasters, their contact phone numbers.

I was soon to discover that ORBO's responsibilities extended beyond the provision of religious programmes for the World Service. Our department was also regarded as an occasional resource for several of the other 37 different language sections in the External Services. I even sometimes, despite my lay status, found myself acting as a kind of chaplain to the staff.

My first learning experience came on my first day in the office. Having been introduced to Sheena Stewart, my competent secretary, who had drawn up for me a chart of the schedules I would need to observe, and Ronald Farrow, my colleague, who was experienced as a producer and religious broadcaster himself, I sent them both off for lunch while I familiarized myself with the various files in the office. At that moment the phone rang. It was from the news room. 'We're covering the story of the Pope's visit to Ireland', said the caller. 'We just want to check whether the Church in Ireland is established or not.' My first reaction was to say, 'No, I'm sure Ireland's a secular state' and the caller rang off. Then I was beset with doubt. I rang the *Irish Times*, but it was lunch time and there was no-one to deal with the call. The time for the news bulletin came and it was too late for me to make any further enquiries. I pushed all doubts to the back of my mind until they came back to haunt me in the early hours of the morning. Then I turned on the radio and heard the measured voice of the World Service news reader saying, 'Pope John Paul II has today been visiting Ireland, which is a secular state'. I breathed a sigh of relief, thinking I must have got it right, only to realize later that in fact I had been the authority on which that information was based! Fortunately it was correct, but I learned then how important it is always to know the source of information as well as its substance.

It was clear that I needed instruction in BBC procedures and programme guidelines as well as training in the art and the mechanics of radio production. I was sent on a couple of courses to the Langham, the building opposite Broadcasting House which had once been a luxurious hotel accommodating distinguished visitors to the great Empire Exhibition of 1851 (and which has since been restored to its former glory). During the war it had fallen into disuse and was temporarily being used as a training centre for the BBC. We apprentices were turned loose in its studios and among its equipment under the strict and skilled supervision of experienced producers and sound engineers.

I stood in awe at first of our tutors, all of whom had long experience in radio, like Doreen Forsyth, whom I had first met when she was a producer of *Woman's Hour*, a programme regarded as a model of good production. She was a formidable teacher, demanding high standards, but also greatly encouraging. Then I learned that she was a Methodist who confessed that she had been equally apprehensive about meeting me! We became personally good friends and have been so ever since. I was assigned to several specific modules of training, focusing on using the spoken word – writing links, editing tape, interviewing, chairing a radio discussion, blending music with speech, preparing documentary material, directing dramatized features and producing outside broadcasts, all of which would come within my orbit as

ORBO. We had skilled technicians on hand to instruct us in microphone technique and in the use of the ubiquitous and heavy UHER tape recording machines which in those days presented an occupational hazard to interviewers and reporters! I had not realized before how many different skills are involved in the art of radio production. The courses proved to be not only hard work but a lot of fun too, especially as a member of one of them was the aspiring comic writer Jimmy Mulville, who kept us cheerful despite any disastrous mistakes we made.

I was soon back in the office and in the studios for real. Our regular religious output on the World Service in those days was extensive. Every day, following immediately after the 8 am GMT news bulletin and repeated twice during the day and night, we broadcast a recorded four-minute talk called *Reflections,* which, like the live *Thought for the Day* on Radio 4, was intended to be a comment on a matter of faith related to a current issue. In view of the different time zones in which *Reflections* would be heard, last-minute changes sometimes had to be made in the light of a developing news story.

Again it was a story concerning the Pope that presented me with one of my greatest challenges. At 5.30 one evening I was just preparing to go home from Bush House, knowing that *Reflections* for the rest of the day had been well taken care of, when the phone rang and again it was from the news room. 'News has just come through that the Pope has been shot', they announced. 'There are no details yet of the extent of the injuries.' I decided immediately that for the rest of the day *Reflections* must be replaced by broadcast prayers for the Pope, which I then recorded personally for all the remaining slots. It was suggested to me that we should also prepare immediately an appropriate broadcast for use in the sad eventuality that the wounds proved to be fatal. Both recordings were left in the continuity studio and I was assured that as the story developed overnight, the relevant tape would be played. I was encouraged to go home and trust my colleagues to look after the matter, but I had a sleepless night, worrying lest the wrong tape were used. Mercifully, those prayers and many others across the world were heard and the Pope's life was spared!

As well as daily *Reflections* we produced a regular weekly magazine programme called *Report on Religion* which Ronald Farrow presented and which we prepared together. We drew our material mainly from religious news items coming from the world-wide agencies and from many of our 20 overseas correspondents (all of whom incidentally in those days were men). We also used some material repeated from the weekly *Sunday* programme on Radio 4. Monitoring the latter for possible use, I soon learned how different are the requirements of programmes designed for a 'domestic' audience from those to be broadcast internationally. The audience we were broadcasting to was ecumenical in the fullest sense of having world-wide concerns and embracing a wide diversity of faiths. In fact I was even asked on one occasion to prepare for the Chinese language services a 100-word explanation of the major differences between the Christian denominations in Britain, for translation into Mandarin for the benefit of listeners in China.

Moreover, to this world-wide audience religion was a live topic and generated a considerable amount of correspondence. So I was often called upon to take part in the weekly programme *Postmark Africa* which dealt with queries from listeners throughout the African continent about abstruse questions such as 'How did Joshua manage to make the sun stand still?' or 'What is meant by a venial sin?'

I received one extraordinarily puzzling letter from a school teacher in India who wanted to know where in the Bible there is any reference to ice-cream. He assured me that he had heard a speaker on the World Service quoting two biblical references to ice-cream and he wanted to share them with the children in his school. I was completely puzzled and having searched through all *Reflections* scripts over several months, could find no such reference. One day over lunch with colleagues I mentioned this fact, when light dawned on the face of Iain Thomas, Sports Organiser, who remembered that, recently in a rainy interval during a Test Match commentary, Brian Johnston had entertained his audience with riddles: 'Where is ice-cream mentioned in the Bible? Answer: In the Lyons of Judah and the Walls of Jericho!' So I now had the difficult job of explaining to a listener in India that this was all a joke and that Walls and Lyons were well-known ice-cream manufacturers in Britain. Such are the pitfalls of attempts at humour in international broadcasting.

One broadcaster receiving a large post bag in those days was the Revd Austen Williams, vicar of St Martin in the Fields, which was regarded almost as the parish church of the World Service. We broadcast services from there once a month, and Austen's deep velvet voice became as familiar to our listeners as views of the church standing in Trafalgar Square. The programme was always recorded at an actual evening service, where Ronald or I would sit in a small studio in the bowels of St Martin's and edit the tape for broadcast later. If it were a particularly wet evening there was often a larger congregation, as many of the tramps congregating around St Martin's would come in for shelter, and we sometimes had to edit out the sound of their snores during the service! On one occasion one shouted out blasphemies during the benediction, so we had to ask Austen to repeat it. Unfortunately in editing the tape I missed a few inches, so an astonished World Service audience heard the vicar closing the service by saying, 'If you give me the green light, I'll give you a blessing.'

In addition to our regular weekly and daily broadcasts we were also invited to offer documentary and feature programmes to be included in the general World Service schedules. These had to be submitted along with suggestions from other programme areas to Anthony Rendell, the World Service Editor, and his colleague Ian Gillham, Head of World Service Productions. They would discuss our ideas with us, offer helpful suggestions and advise us as to how our contributions if accepted would fit into the overall pattern and total budget of the schedule. They would also preside over a critical review to which some of our programmes would eventually be submitted along with those of colleagues in other departments. A lively discussion arose in the reviewing group itself over a series of dialogue programmes we ran concerning some of the controversial theological issues of the time under the title, *Believe It or Not,* when we invited people from opposing points of view to argue between them. For instance, the Rt Revd David Jenkins who was at that time Bishop of Durham, was asked to debate with the Rt Revd Graham Leonard, Bishop of London, what each understood by the phrase 'the physical resurrection' of Christ. There were similar dialogues about other current issues such as the ordination of women, the authority of Scripture and whether the Kingdom of God could be equated with any one political system rather than another.

Among the most memorable programmes we produced was a series of inter-faith discussions called *Words of Faith.* They involved a rabbi, an imam, a Christian minister and a Hindu priest. As we worked together in the same team over several weeks we came to know one another well. It was interesting to note how different alliances formed between us according to the particular word we were discussing. For example, the word 'mission' was regarded as an admirable aim by both Muslim and Christian, but the Jew and the Hindu gave it low priority in their concerns. The concept of the 'incarnation' of God was totally unacceptable to both Jew and Muslim but it was completely comprehensible to both Hindu and Christian. When the Christian eagerly pointed out that the Christian view of Christ's incarnation is that it was unique, the Hindu quietly and politely responded, 'But we believe every incarnation of God is unique!'

The most unifying word shared between us was the word 'prayer'. I invited each panel member to introduce into the studio some sound associated in their faith with the ritual of prayer. As the studio was filled successively with the sound of the *shofar*, of the *muezzin*, of a large gong and of church bells there followed a reverent stillness and a profound sense of all of us sharing in the same human aspiration toward a power and a Spirit beyond ourselves.

The motto of the BBC is the prophetic-sounding text, 'Nation shall speak peace unto nation'. I felt that it was equally important that faith should speak peace to faith. So we encouraged broadcasters from many different faiths to take part in all our programmes. As it was still rare in those days to hear speakers from other faiths contributing regularly to the religious output on domestic radio I found an interesting aspect of my job was spotting broadcasting talent and increasing the number and diversity of contributors to our *Reflections*. Rabbi Hugo Gryn became a most popular broadcaster, and, like most rabbis, had a fund of good stories to tell. Yusuf Islam gave a most moving testimony describing his personal search for peace and his eventual conversion to Islam, ending with extracts from the Koran chanted in Arabic in that same melodic, haunting voice we had known in his days of fame as the pop singer, Cat Stevens. I encouraged a young Sikh journalist named Inderjit Singh to become a regular contributor. He has since become one of the longest running contributors to *Thought for the Day* on Radio 4, which also now includes more regularly participants from various faiths.

We were fortunate that many of 'the great and the good' agreed to contribute to *Reflections* by giving us four-minute meditations on their own favourite texts, which came from an interesting variety of sources. It was a privilege to be invited into the gracious home of the great violinist Yehudi Menuhin, who shared with us his love of the wisdom of Lao-tse in the ancient Chinese collection of sayings known as the *Tao te Ching* . He read from a well-worn German translation which he told us had been given him 35 years before by one of his accompanists. He chose as one of his favourite quotations, 'Soft and delicate are the ways of life; hard and stiff is the way of death'. In the Speaker's House above the Houses of Parliament, Lord George Thomas spoke of his appreciation of the psalms which he had known since his childhood. In the House of Lords, Lord Fenner Brockway quoted words Bernard Shaw had said to him when he was a teenager and he had asked the great dramatist what he should do with his life. The reply was: 'Find out what the life force, the creative force in your time is making for and you make for it too.' The veteran prison visitor and campaigner for penal reform Lord Longford chose as his favourite text the words of Jesus, 'People who are well do not need a doctor, but only those who are sick. I have not come to call respectable people, but outcasts.'

With some apprehension I accepted an invitation to go down into Sussex to record texts chosen by the distinguished broadcaster Malcolm Muggeridge, by then retired and recently converted to Christian faith. Memories of earlier clashes with him during debates on television haunted me. I was so nervous that, having invited him to speak, as he did fluently without notes for exactly the required four minutes, I discovered to my utter chagrin that I had forgotten to turn on the UHER tape recorder. But he and Kitty his wife were most patient and, after a break for afternoon tea, he spontaneously gave me three more *Reflections,* each based on texts from the Gospels, about which he testified:

---

In the words of the Gospel and in the great drama of our Lord's ministry and crucifixion and resurrection I have found the words of eternal life . . . I've been a journalist all my life, writing about what's going on in the world and I see Jesus overcoming the world by making us understand what is reality.[1]

I felt that I was fortunate in that, during my time at the World Service, the heads of both the major Christian communities in this country were excellent communicators, always ready to co-operate with plans I discussed with them. So at the time of the great Christian festivals or other national occasions I knew that both Archbishop Runcie and Cardinal Basil Hume were ready to give time to us at Bush House, as well as answering the many demands made upon them by all the other media. We were invited on several occasions to Lambeth Palace where we came to know the staff well. The archbishop's chaplain, the Revd Richard Chartres, now Bishop of London, took to the microphone willingly as a contributor to *Reflections*, saying that when he came to Bush House, it reminded him of George V addressing the Empire! I teasingly suggested to him that despite his own sonorous voice and impressive appearance, we didn't really want him to sound imperial!

Cardinal Hume used often to walk along the embankment from Westminster to Bush House, and when he arrived he always found time to talk to the receptionists and commissionaires on his way to the studios. On one occasion when we were recording the cardinal's meditations for Holy Week, we kept being interrupted by the noise of hammering somewhere in the vicinity, a sound all too frequently penetrating the studios at Bush House. In embarrassment I apologized for asking the cardinal to repeat his message. He graciously smiled and said, 'I thought for a moment you were trying to include sound effects for Good Friday'!

---

1 'Texts for Today' scripts recorded by Malcolm Muggeridge, 1983.

Terry Waite, the Archbishop of Canterbury's envoy, agreed to take part in a new programme series I was introducing. It was called *A Month in a Monastery* and was a kind of ecclesiastical adaptation of the ever popular *Desert Island Discs*. We asked contributors to imagine that they were faced with spending a month in silent, solitary retreat. They would be allowed to choose one book, one record and one person who could visit them on one day during the month. Our first contributor was Dame Judi Dench, who charmed us with her memories of her own spiritual search and who spoke in warm gratitude about the Roman Catholic priest who had ministered to her and her husband Michael Williams on the eve of their marriage. Our second contributor was Terry Waite, whose broadcast in this series seemed chillingly prophetic. Shortly after making it, he was kidnapped in Lebanon and disappeared from our sight and knowledge for over four long years. In that anxious time when people were still praying for him, I used to play the recording of his programme often in church services, recalling what he had said about the things he hoped would sustain him in a time of solitariness. He had spoken of how he would need to begin a journey different from all the others he had ever undertaken – a journey inwards, during which he believed he would come to a deeper knowledge of himself and a firmer faith in God. Imagine our joy when we heard that at last he had been released, and when we even had a phone call from him saying that in the last few months when he finally had access to a radio, he had heard our daily *Reflections* and had been able to share in worship through listening to our church services.

Although this was still long before the era of e-mails we encouraged audience participation as much as possible by inviting people to write to us, choosing their favourite hymns, and telling us the reason for their choice. *Sunday Half Hour*, which we recorded from domestic radio, was a top favourite among our programmes, and requests for hymns came from all parts of the globe, including one cablegram which simply said, 'Any hymn by Charles Wesley for the Fijian contingent in the UN peacekeeping force in the Lebanon!'

The year 1982 marked the Silver Jubilee of the External Services. We held a special thanksgiving service in St Martin in the Fields, broadcast on the World Service. It began with a haunting introit composed by Barry Rose as a setting to the text, 'Nation shall speak peace unto nation'. The Revd Prebendary Kennedy Bell (a former ORBO) directed the St Martin singers in the anthem: 'Their sound has gone out through all the earth'. The current managing Director of the External Services, Mr Douglas Muggeridge, read an extract from the visionary writings of Lord Reith, founder of the BBC, entitled *Broadcast over Britain*. The Chairman of the Governors, Mr George Howard, read from the prophet Micah and the Revd Colin Semper, who was by this time Provost of Coventry cathedral, preached the sermon. I was given the privilege of leading the intercessions and I was particularly pleased that prayers were also offered by staff members of the External Services from the Hindu, Jewish, Christian, Muslim, Sikh and Buddhist traditions.

As part of the Jubilee celebrations, a new venture was launched. Douglas Muggeridge as Managing Director agreed to take part in an international phone-in. This was an experiment in international broadcasting and there was at first considerable anxiety as to how it would work and whether anyone would actually phone in. But its success encouraged the Editor of World Service to embark on a whole series in which listeners would be given the opportunity to speak personally on the phone to world leaders in many different spheres of life. It was decided to begin by inviting the Archbishop of Canterbury to take part. I was asked to be on the end of in-coming calls as an editor selecting which questions to put through to the Archbishop. We were kept fully occupied for the whole duration of the programme, with lively questions coming from all parts of the world. From then on, World Service phone-ins became a popular series featuring many world statesmen and women. The format was copied later in a similar series put out by Voice of America.

The World Service had for many years broadcast the special service held annually in March to mark Commonwealth Day. By the Queen's permission it was held in Westminster Abbey and included prayers from all the major faiths, which in those days would still not have been permitted in most churches. One of my most challenging and interesting experiences in broadcasting was giving a commentary on that colourful service, attended by representatives of the nations of the former British Empire, all wearing national dress. From a precarious perch up in the rafters of Westminster Abbey I had to try to identify the various dignitaries and recognize their national flags.

I always felt that working at Bush House was a rare privilege. It was like being at the hub of world events with an international team of colleagues whose knowledge of their own particular areas of the world was well informed and, in the best traditions of the BBC, as unbiased as it was possible to be. A commemorative booklet published at the time of the Jubilee spelt out the history of the External Services which, like so many British institutions, seems to have come into being almost by chance. From the start Lord Reith, the visionary founder of the British Broadcasting Company, had seen the possibilities of radio as a means of international communication. But that had to wait until short-wave broadcasting could be developed, which required extra expenditure. The Government declared that it had no intention of paying for such a service. Lord Reith at first also refused to meet the cost, saying it was unfair to expect licence payers in Britain to fund programmes they would never be able to hear. Eventually, however, the BBC agreed to pay the initial cost of a service to the Empire. A new transmitter was built at Daventry and on Christmas Day 1932 King George V broadcast his first message to the Empire: 'Through one of the marvels of modern science I am enabled this Christmas day to speak to all my peoples throughout the Empire . . . I speak now from my home and from my heart to you all, to men and women so cut off by the snows and the deserts or the seas that only voices out of the air can reach them . . .'

A couple of years later, Italian stations began broadcasting in Arabic in support of the invasion of Ethiopia. The British Government decided that Britain too must start broadcasting in Arabic and other foreign languages. Lord Reith argued that only the BBC had the expertise to undertake such a development. He insisted that if the Government wanted foreign language broadcasts it would have to pay for them, but he insisted equally firmly that in these broadcasts the BBC should be editorially independent of the Government. 'Prestige', he argued 'depended on broadcasting that was both truthful and comprehensive'.[2] In 1937, shortly before the outbreak of the Second World War, he was quoted as saying, 'The BBC would be trusted where the Government might not be.'

Throughout the war years, when the BBC was a source of hope and inspiration to millions in Nazi-occupied Europe, it gained a reputation for honesty and truthfulness in contrast to the blatant propaganda which was a clear part of Nazi and Fascist strategy. Later, for 50 years, behind the Iron Curtain the BBC was still regarded by many clandestine listeners as a reliable and independent source of information. (I was amused when one of our correspondents told me how, during a visit to Albania, which was still at

2 *Voice for the World: 50 Years of Broadcasting to the World, 1932–1982*, BBC External Services Publicity Unit, 1982, p. 7.

that time a militantly atheistic state, he had met a government official who had casually referred in discussion to something he had heard said on *Reflections* only a few days before.)

There was a time when people thought of the World Service as broadcasting primarily to those living within the British Empire who spoke English and particularly to expatriate Britons. This had long ceased to be a priority. During John Tusa's period as Managing Director of World Service (1986–92), an audience survey revealed that of the 25 million listeners reckoned to tune in regularly to World Service broadcasts the majority had English as their second language. 'Short wave broadcasting', as John Tusa described it, 'is in essence anarchic – it leaps boundaries and scatters forbidden thoughts and challenges otherwise unchallenge-able authorities.'[3]

Though funded by Government grants, all the External Services have always insisted on freedom from Government editorial con-trol. The Foreign Office can determine what languages the BBC broadcasts in, but it has no say in the content of the programmes broadcast in those languages. During my years at Bush House that independence and impartiality came under particular strain at the time of the outbreak of the war over the Falkland Islands. Ironically, as a result of one of the many Government surveys as to where cuts could be made in the budget of the External Services, it had been decided that the Spanish speaking service to Europe should be closed down from March 1982. On 2 April 1982 Argentine forces occupied Port Stanley on the Falkland Islands and within days the BBC was asked to expand its transmissions in Spanish to Latin America.

Throughout the Falklands war there was conflict between the media and the Ministry of Defence about the restrictions to be

---

3  John Tusa, *Conversations with the World*, BBC Books, 1990.

imposed on the way events were reported. At one point the BBC transmitter on Ascension Island was commandeered by the Ministry to set up its own station, but in spite of that and of the fact that BBC broadcasts were jammed (not very effectively) by the Argentine authorities, audiences of the Latin American Service continued to grow. The BBC correspondent Brian Hanrahan managed skilfully to avoid giving away too many restricted facts in what became his famous phrase describing the effects of British air attacks: 'I counted them all out and I counted them all back.'

'The Falklands war', wrote John Tusa, 'put BBC principles to the test . . . Truth does not need to be the first casualty in war – it is often the great survivor.' He quotes a Caribbean listener who is reported to have said concerning the BBC's coverage of the war, 'You couldn't tell which side they were on!'[4]

For those of us in the Religious Department one comparatively minor anxiety during the Falklands War was how this was likely to affect the plans of the Pope to visit the United Kingdom. We had made extensive arrangements for covering his visit on the World Service as also had our colleagues in many of the language services. The Pope kept to his original full itinerary and arrived at Gatwick airport on 28 May 1982. As was to be expected his message was a plea for a peaceful resolution of the conflict in the South Atlantic, which was drawing near to its close.

From an ecumenical and ecclesiastical point of view the highlight of the Pope's visit was when he joined the Archbishop of Canterbury for prayer in Canterbury Cathedral. The Pope recalled that it had been the vision of Pope Gregory that had sent St Augustine as an apostle to England. Now after centuries of division he rejoiced in the growing dialogue between the churches. Together with the Anglican archbishop and the leaders of the other

---

4 John Tusa, *Conversations with the World*, BBC Books, 1990.

main churches in the UK, he declared, 'On this eve of Pentecost we commit ourselves to the task of working for unity with firmer faith, renewed hope and even deeper love.'

Bishop Trevor Huddleston, in one of his frequent contributions to our inter-faith discussions on the World Service, once said, 'Archbishop Temple called the coming together of the churches "the great new fact of the twentieth century". For me', he went on to say, 'it has become the great old bore of our time. The far more exciting ecumenism is the coming together of the faiths.'

So I was happy when we had the responsibility of broadcasting also the gathering of the world's religious leaders, at Assisi, in 1986 for an 'Earth summit' at the invitation of Pope John Paul II. Again, I had to face an interesting query from the news room. 'In a press release,' said one of the journalists, ' it reports that the Pope has called the leaders of the world faiths together for prayer, but there's a footnote which says, "Please note, this does not mean he is calling them to pray together." Can you please explain to me theologically the difference?' I had to confess that we were still walking on tentative ground where inter-faith prayer is concerned. Yet we had learned during the past few years to pray together as Christians in the one world Church, however great our differences. I believed we were now reaching a new awareness of the importance of humanity learning to pray with one voice in our shared concern for the preservation of our environment and for the future peace of our world. It was always my hope that 'faith speaking to faith' in our broadcasting could be an important contribution to 'nation speaking peace to nation'.

My own days at Bush House were, regrettably for me, coming to an end. The BBC has a clear policy of retirement at the age of 60. So in June 1987 I was treated to the traditional retirement party and presented with the customary autograph book with goodwill messages from colleagues. Sheena had gone to the trouble of inviting everyone who had shared in our *Reflections* or our dialogue programmes to add their signatures. It gave me great joy to have these messages from people of so many different faiths and nationalities whom it had been my privilege to come to know as friends during my tenure at Bush House. Most intriguing of all was a note from one of my colleagues in the World Service – 'Gone today, and here tomorrow!' which proved to be prophetic of what still lay ahead of me.

# 10

# *Worship with the World*

۶ﷻﺀ

One commitment I had been permitted to continue through-out my period of service at Bush House was my membership of the Central Committee of the World Council of Churches. This was seen as not detracting from my responsibilities as ORBO. The continued opportunities of travel it brought provided me with plenty of material for *Report on Religion*, for documentary features and for interviews with some of the leading personalities on the world-wide ecumenical scene.

In 1981 the Central Committee met in Dresden. It was fasci-nating to see at first hand what was happening in the churches in what was still then known as the German Democratic Republic. We could almost sense early vibrations of the protest movement which at the end of the decade was to bring many thousands of young East Germans into the churches and eventually out on to the streets until in 1988, like the walls of Jericho, the infamous Berlin Wall would be brought tumbling down.

The Central Committee was welcomed to Dresden in a majestic service of worship in the bomb-damaged cathedral thronged with thousands of worshippers and throbbing to the music of a mighty organ, a massed choir and trumpeters. Clearly the Christians of East Germany, most of whom were not permitted to travel beyond their own borders, rejoiced in the opportunity of meeting repre-sentatives of the 300 member churches of the World Council who had come from countries right across the world.

I was able to present to the committee on behalf of the Programme to Combat Racism a report entitled *Justice for Aboriginal Australians* written by a small, international group in co-operation with colleagues in the Australian Council of Churches. As a direct outcome of the Conference on World Mission and Evangelism held in Melbourne in 1980 we had been invited to spend three weeks visiting and listening to communities of aboriginal people across the continent. Colleagues from Australian Broadcasting accompanied us on most of our visits. They recorded the interviews and discussions through which we came to learn something of aboriginal history and spirituality and also the extent of the medical and social needs of this deprived section of Australian society.

As aboriginal people shared with us the spiritual insights enshrined in their traditional heritage, we came to realize that their struggle to survive as a people is not only a political and economic struggle but a deeply religious one too. 'We do not say the land belongs to us,' said one elder, 'but we belong to the land.' With that belonging comes a profound sense of stewardship. In one discussion people were resisting pressure from a mining company who were offering financial compensation in return for permission to mine for uranium in aboriginal ancestral land. One old woman warned them, 'Our dreaming tells us of a monster dwelling beneath the earth who will destroy those who disturb its peace. What do you want to do with your uranium – destroy the earth?'

I personally was humbled and haunted by the words of one aboriginal Christian woman whose children had been taken from her many years before in the mistaken and prejudiced assumption that it would be better for them to be brought up in a children's home and given the benefits of 'white' education. She herself had no security of tenure in the place where she was living and the community to which she belonged had been scattered and dispossessed of their land. She said in an interview, 'We cried to the Lord in our trouble for someone to hear us. We believe he has sent you people to tell the world that those things which have been hidden must be made known.' It made me realize that broadcasting is in many ways a sacred vocation. The report was commended for distribution to churches throughout the world and for referral to the United Nations. It received widespread coverage in the press and brought concern for indigenous peoples high on to the agenda of the World Council of Churches.

Within the meetings of the Dresden central committee many issues of world-wide concern were debated. The immediately current news of the latest developments in the neutron bomb nerved the committee to issue an uncompromising condemnation of all nuclear weapons and to call churches throughout the world to work for peace and disarmament. On issues such as these the central committee managed to reach almost total unanimity.

The storms that rocked the ecumenical boat were internal rather than external. The major storm was the least expected. It was provoked by the report from the conference that had been recently held in Sheffield on the Community of Women and Men in the Church, bringing together reports and recommendations from groups all over the world. They had been participating in a WCC study programme which was more widely supported and more fully reported than any other ecumenical project of its kind. Its summary report called for equal participation of women and men in all areas of church life, a proposal that was regarded by some as posing a threat to ecumenism. Orthodox representatives refused to endorse a letter written at the Sheffield Conference expressing the pain of women denied the possibility of offering for the priesthood.

But, as Bishop Schönherr, head of the Evangelical Churches of East Germany, commented during a boat trip on the River Elbe, the ecumenical ship was used to navigating dangerous waters. Our journey up river was a kind of acted parable of the church's situation in a communist state, as we made slow progress against the tide, veering at times from one side to another. On the banks on both sides of the river local congregations gathered to wave us on our way, accompanied by brass bands as they sang their hymns of praise.

The next year, 1982, the Central Committee met in Geneva, at a time of crisis in the Middle East. Following the massacre of Palestinian civilians in the Sabra and Shatila refugee camps in Lebanon, Beirut had become caught up in an intensifying civil war. From their headquarters in the most stricken area of West Beirut, the staff of the Middle East Council of Churches with their Muslim neighbours were doing a heroic task of relief work. It was immediately decided to send an ecumenical team to visit the member churches in Lebanon, expressing solidarity with the suffering people and exploring how best the international community could be of assistance. Archbishop Sundby of Sweden, Jacques Maury of the French Reformed Church and Bishop Maximos of the Eastern Orthodox Church agreed at a moment's notice to go to what was a dangerous situation. Their visit meant a lot to the little known Christian communities in Lebanon and to the Middle East Council of Churches. The horrific report they brought back received wide publicity throughout the world's media. This was active ecumenism at its best.

Within the work of the World Council itself, there had been exciting development in the area of Faith and Order. We had before us the agreed text on *Baptism, Eucharist and Ministry* which had been arrived at after a long process of consultation with theologians of every hue across the world. Heralded as an 'ecumenical breakthrough' it demonstrated that it is possible to reach common understanding on the three great issues which have been regarded in the past as stumbling blocks on the way to unity.

A large amount of time at this central committee was taken up with plans being made for the next Assembly of the World Council of Churches scheduled to be held in Vancouver in 1983. I had been asked to chair the Assembly Planning Committee which entailed yet more travelling for me. Not only did I need to visit Vancouver itself to meet and work with the committees responsible for the local arrangements, but it was also suggested that I should take part in two pre-Assembly visits to meet with some of the delegates who would be coming to an Assembly for the first time.

My first visit was to an area of the world new to me, north-east Asia. We were invited to meet with the delegates who would be coming to Vancouver from churches in Hong Kong, Japan and Taiwan. The churches in Hong Kong were facing with great uncertainty the approaching end of an era, when the British Government was due to hand over sovereignty to China in 15 years' time. Apart from the tourist-dazzling shops and bargain markets, we saw a frenzy of new building going on with high-rise blocks of flats springing up to house the thousands of low-income workers flooding into Hong Kong from Vietnam and China. We were impressed by the Christian Industrial Mission working with community action groups seeking to defend the workers' rights. We noted the contrast between the pessimism of some of the church leaders as they regarded the future with apprehension, and the optimism of many of the younger generation looking forward to the ending of British rule. When we went up into the New Territories right on the border with China we caught a glimpse of the mainland itself. It struck me that the people we met from the Hong Kong Council of Churches seemed to have as yet little information about or contact with the Chinese churches, who were still to come fully into the ecumenical movement.

Our journey took us on to Tokyo, where we were joined by delegates who would be going to the Assembly from Korea, Taiwan and Hong Kong, together with the small delegation from the United Church of Christ in Japan. We were the guests of the Christian Lay Academy in the seaside resort of Oiso where we had magnificent views of Mt Fuji. From the moment I left my shoes on the threshold of the beautifully designed building and entered the spacious but sparsely furnished lounge where a huge TV set was displaying an extraordinary drama, I was aware that we had arrived in a different culture. We were most hospitably welcomed by the Director, Tosh Arai, and served with my first Japanese meal, comprising many different, and to me unfamiliar, kinds of fish.

We were invited to go for a rest in our rooms, after refreshing ourselves with the opportunity of a hot bath. I made the mistake of thinking that a bath was for the purpose of washing oneself and so when I had finished doing that I tried to empty the huge tub of water. Only the next morning did I learn that bath tubs in Japan are meant only for use after a shower, for the purpose of relaxing, alone or in company with others and that the water was meant for all to share! The next evening we were taken as a group to some nearby hot springs where, separated only by bamboo partitions, all of us, men and women, enjoyed splashing about in the water and then going together to a nearby hostelry for a meal and a lively international karaoke session.

Most of our time in the Academy was spent discussing the theme and programme of the Assembly and ways in which those who spoke little English might be helped to participate. Language is always the great problem in an international gathering. Although the World Council provides simultaneous translation in English, German, French and Spanish, the fact that all these are Western languages puts people from other continents and cultures at a grave disadvantage. It was not only the question of language that our hosts raised with us. They were also eager that the experience of Christians living as minority communities in their own countries would be understood by churches in other parts of the world. Japanese Christians spoke movingly of what they had learned through sharing their nation's shame and also its suffering. They described how the churches had resisted government attempts to rewrite history by obliterating from school text books all mention of Japanese atrocities and defeat. One of the Japanese delegates had just returned from addressing a conference in Hiroshima on the subject of disarmament. I was grateful that he and several other delegates agreed to be interviewed for *Report on Religion.*

The Presbyterian Church in Taiwan was the strongest of the churches we visited in north east Asia. This too is a minority group in comparison with the nation's total population. Yet it comes under heavy pressure from the nationalist government because it is mainly a Taiwanese organization and as such is seen as a threat to the Chinese majority living in proud independence of the main-land. The American leader of the 'International Council of Christians', Carl McIntyre, a vociferous opponent of the WCC, had also been warning the church in Taiwan against what he called the 'communist' influence in the ecumenical movement.

Nevertheless we were enthusiastically received by our hosts, who took us on a fascinating sight-seeing tour in the capital, Taipei. There we visited the massive Chiang Kai Shek mausoleum and the Imperial Palace Museum, full of artefacts from ancient China that were seized and carried over from the mainland at the time of the revolution. Wherever we went in Taiwan there was a sense of the hovering presence of the nationalist government. We were warned that we were probably under surveillance throughout our visit.

We travelled by train across the island, going south to Taichung where we met a group of enthusiastic evangelists who told us about their mission among the hill peoples, which increased government suspicion of the church. We were disappointed that when we went on to Tainan to visit the theological college there, we just missed attending worship in the chapel and the opportunity of addressing the students. But we did overhear the closing anthem in the service. The singing was superb and when I expressed my disappointment at not having had the opportunity to record such an excellent choir, the principal immediately called the whole choir back again. They recorded for me three Christmas carols, one English, one Chinese and one Taiwanese, all of which were so beautifully sung that we were able to include them in a Christmas celebration on the BBC World Service.

My one disappointment in Taiwan was that I was not permitted to visit the courageous General Secretary of the Presbyterian Church, Dr Kao, who was in gaol serving a seven-year prison sentence for having given pastoral help to a political fugitive. His wife came to see me and passed on a message from him saying, 'Please do not worry about my suffering, but pray that I may carry on my ministry here in gaol.' She told me that there were three men in his cell which was about 15 feet by 6 feet, with no furniture, bed or table. But he had said to his companions, 'Let us not think of this as a prison but as a school. Here we will learn about human beings and how we can live together.' On such strong faith is the Church in Taiwan and indeed the ecumenical movement built.

We had learned something of the cost of such faith even within the group of us who had been working together on the programme for the Vancouver Assembly. The theme chosen was *Jesus Christ, the Life of the World*. In one of our committee meetings in 1981 we had been exploring all the possible ways of treating the theme. What was meant by the word 'Life'? One of our members was Bishop Samuel of the Coptic Orthodox Church in Egypt. He had adamantly insisted that we must in at least one session consider what Christians believe about life after death, an important issue of faith for many Christians facing persecution in today's world. Some weeks after this discussion I was watching television at home when I saw on the news bulletin the picture of Bishop Samuel standing on a podium close beside President Sadat to whom he always gave loyal support despite the fact that they were of different faiths. Then, to my horror, I saw shots fired and both President Sadat and Bishop Samuel fell to the ground, victims of the assassin's bullets.

It seemed all the more important that the question of inter-faith relations must have a high place on our agenda at Vancouver and that guests coming from other faith communities should be made to feel not only welcome but valued for the contribution they could bring to our deliberations. So we gratefully accepted an invitation from Archbishop Trevor Huddleston, whose province at that time spanned the Indian Ocean, to hold a preparatory inter-faith consultation on the assembly theme in Mauritius, an island with a long tradition of inter-faith dialogue and harmony. Thousands of people of many faiths shared annually in a pilgrimage honouring the memory of the folk hero Père Laval, a saintly French priest who had made his home among the indentured Indian labourers working in the sugar fields. Hindus, Muslims, Buddhists and Christians all traditionally came together to exchange gestures of peace as twelve baskets of white doves were released to fly over the heads of the whole assembled crowd.

In the course of our meeting in this tropical paradise of an island we listened to papers read by Buddhist, Hindu, Jewish, Muslim, Sikh and Christian theologians as well as representatives of traditional religions in Africa and of the native peoples of Canada. All spoke on their understanding of the theme *The Meaning of Life.* What struck me was the convergence in so much of what they were saying. We all affirmed the dignity and mystery of human life in its fullness and recognized its relation to some kind of ultimate reality. We shared a concern for justice, compassion and hope in a world beset with injustice, indifference and despair.

In between listening to and discussing papers we came to know one another well on a personal level and at the kind of depth which can stand the strain of honest confrontation. Honesty is as important in true dialogue as sincerity and acceptance. There was an occasion, for example, when relationships between our Jewish participants and a Palestinian Christian living in the occupied territory in the West Bank were strained almost to breaking point. We were all compelled to recognize the pain inflicted on 'the other' but also to acknowledge the sins committed by the communities to which we ourselves belonged.

While not being expected to worship together we were invited each day to observe each other's various and separate ways of worship. We attended as onlookers and eavesdroppers but the reverence of the different rituals had such a deep effect upon us that some who came only to watch found themselves wanting to worship. I for one was happy to participate when I was invited by Art Solomon of the Objibway nation of Canada to savour the scent of the smoke of smouldering sage and cedar which he offered up like incense. I was impressed by the fact that Muslims always pray as members of a community, using the plural pronoun 'we' and never presenting themselves alone before God. I found Buddhist chanting a calming of the mind and the Hindu 'puja' with its offerings of flowers and fruits a feast for the eyes. Our Sikh participant introduced us to a treasury of most beautiful prayers. A Christian of the Eastern Orthodox tradition opened my mind to a much wider understanding of the breadth of the Holy Spirit's activity when he said: 'The Spirit has always been at work in all humanity everywhere and at all times, giving deep experiences of reality and its meaning to people in all cultures and climes. Insofar as people have responded positively to the work of the Spirit, they have experienced unity with all.'[1]

While I was in Mauritius I had the opportunity of recording our visits to a Buddhist temple, to a Hindu festival and to a synagogue for use in a feature on ways of worship in the different faiths which we later broadcast on the World Service. I was also able to include extracts from an extraordinary service of shared worship held in the cathedral, which the Roman Catholic priest had opened to people of all faiths. Even within the Mass he would regularly include references to any of the special festivals of other faiths such as Divali, Eid, the Chinese New Year or Passover. I suppose some would see in this a danger of syncretism; others would regard it as a sign of solidarity. A local resident in Mauritius said in an interview: 'With a million people of so many different origins living so close to one another in such a confined space, we just have to learn to live together in respect for one another's religions.'

In our message to the Assembly from the Mauritius multi-faith consultation we wrote: 'Steps towards Christian unity cannot be taken as if one first achieved Christian unity and then moved on from there. Christian unity must be sought while at the same time seeking unity wherever possible with others.'[2]

I was glad to meet up again in Vancouver a few months later with the 15 guests from other faiths who had now become such good friends through our shared experience in Mauritius. Among other familiar faces which I recognized among those gathering at the campus of the University of British Columbia were the delegates we had come to know in the Far East and were now able to welcome to the far West! I personally was accompanied to the

---

1 Metropolitan Paulus Gregorius, quoted in *The Meaning of Life: Multi-faith Consultation Mauritius*, WCC, 1983, p.10.
2 Ibid., p.12.

Assembly by several friends and colleagues. The BBC sent a team of both radio and television staff to record some of the sessions and particularly the worship which promised to be a distinctive feature of this particular Assembly. It was to be held in an enormous marquee marked by splendid white and yellow stripes (coincidentally the papal colours) that had been specially erected on the campus for the occasion. As one who had been in on the planning for the Assembly, I knew that this was one of those creative ideas that had arisen out of what at one point seemed like dire necessity.

Our first reconnaissance visit to the campus had not been promising. For one thing, we arrived in a deluge followed by a mist which hid from sight even the famous views of Vancouver bay and the surrounding mountains which make the University of British Columbia one of the most beautifully sited campuses in the world. Our first tour of the premises had not inspired us with great confidence as we trudged along soggy paths between one building and another. There was no place suitable for worship that could accommodate some 4000 people, and the gymnasium, in which we were told the main business sessions would be held, looked like what it was, just a gymnasium with bare walls and a lot of empty space. But the local committees and particularly Gordon How of the Canadian Council of Churches, the Executive Director, did a wonderful job in arranging for the empty walls to be adorned by local artists and designers with superb tapestries and paintings evocative of Canadian scenes and of native Canadian culture. Attractive walkways incorporating symbols of peace, a dominant theme of the Assembly, were designed to link the locations used for the many and various activities within the programme.

A special meditative area among the trees was provided by native Canadians who kept a sacred flame burning there throughout the duration of the Assembly. As a permanent acknowledgment of this world gathering's presence, a group of native carvers presented a 15-metre high totem pole that was erected on the campus and eventually transported to Geneva, to be erected in the grounds of the Ecumenical Institute at Bossey.

The committee responsible for preparing the Assembly's worship came up with the biblically appropriate idea of having a tent as the gathering place. That of itself inevitably influenced the form the worship would take. The use of large symbols and gestures became important where there were few special lighting effects, and the absence of interpreters' booths made it all the more important that hymns and readings should be multilingual. An international team of worship music animators (which included a Latin American, an African, a German and a couple of Canadians) inspired a choir whose singing in the tent became so popular that it set in motion a whole new trend in church music. Lyrics and chants of affirmation from many different cultures came into the repertoire of worship songs used in churches throughout the world. *Kyrie eleison* became a prayer as widely used in the twentieth century as it had been in the first, and the acclamations *Hallelujah* and *Hosanna* needed no translation. It was as though the world Church were rediscovering a universal vernacular of praise.

The opening worship led by Archbishop Scott of Canada was a joyous occasion in which I who had been appointed as the preacher chose as my text the enthusiastic words that tumble out in the opening verses of the first Letter of St John: 'That which we have seen and heard we declare unto you – our theme is the Word of life.' I was aware that for some of the delegates it would still be unusual to hear a woman preach, and I tried in my sermon to reflect on feminine experience of what it means to be able to bear and to nurture life. One of the most moving moments in the service was when representatives brought forward to the altar their most precious symbols of life. Following them an African woman from Zimbabwe brought forward as her gift her own small baby, which Philip Potter gathered into his strong arms in blessing.

Women were to play a larger part in this Assembly than in any previous one, and a special place of rest and relaxation was provided for them in what was called 'The Well', a room which became the centre of much eager conversation as well as valued times of quiet meditation. In the central eucharistic celebration, the Archbishop of Canterbury, Robert Runcie, was flanked by two ordained women from other traditions, one from Denmark and one from Indonesia, among other assistant clergy. Yet this was several years before the Church of England had agreed to the ordination of women priests. The liturgy was the one that had become known as the 'Lima' liturgy, prepared by a Faith and Order Commission meeting at Lima to express the convergence recently achieved between the churches in the study on the subject of *Baptism, Eucharist and the Ministry*.

The galaxy of main speakers included Dorothee Sölle, the radical German theologian, and Jean Vanier, the French Canadian founder of the movement known as *l'Arche* which encourages able and disabled people to live in communities together. Among the most memorable voices we heard were those of powerless people like Darlene Keju Johnson, a young woman from the Marshall Islands. She spoke passionately against the harm being done to women and their unborn babies by the testing of nuclear weapons in that whole area of the Pacific. She described the tumours from which she herself was suffering and from which a few years later she died a premature death.

There is a 'fearful symmetry' (as the poet Michael Roberts described it in a script written for a BBC programme) in the fact that the atomic bomb was dropped on Hiroshima on the date when Christians observe the Feast of the Transfiguration. At Vancouver both events were commemorated on 6 August in a special service of penitence followed by a night-long Prayer Vigil for Peace. This began with one of the Japanese delegates describing what it had been like to be within the vicinity of Hiroshima on the day of the bombing. We were invited to create our own peace symbols out of bits of wire and paper distributed to us. Then suddenly at midnight Desmond Tutu, Bishop of Capetown, arrived. His coming to the Assembly had been delayed by passport difficulties when he tried to leave South Africa. At last he had been able to make the journey and he burst in upon the praying Assembly with the exuberance and confident optimism which the whole world has since come to associate with him.

Not surprisingly therefore, 'justice, peace and the integrity of creation' became a key theme at Vancouver. These three elements were viewed as entry points to a single vision to which the churches were called to make a mutual commitment in a covenant with God and with one another. As the Assembly's message declared emphatically, 'The tree of peace has justice for its roots'. To that biblical concept was added the growing concern for the environment and the new prominence being given to the doctrine of creation and human responsibility towards it. JPIC became the name of a world-wide process which culminated in a major convocation at Seoul in Korea in 1990.

Throughout the Vancouver Assembly I had been kept busy not only on World Council business but also in recording interviews with people from all over the world in response to requests from colleagues in the BBC External Services. We devised an ingenious method whereby presenters of programmes in various language services sent questions to me in Vancouver which I put to people who were present from their areas, recording their answers both in English and in their own language which I then sent back to Bush House for use in the appropriate service.

As someone had predicted at the time of my retirement from

Bush House in 1987, I was soon back broadcasting. Almost immediately after I came out of the doors of Bush House as a staff member of the World Service, I was invited to go through the doors of the Television Centre at White City to discuss a special series of *Songs of Praise* for Christmas which would in fact involve me in another visit to Vancouver.

The idea was for me to present a series of five programmes, taking an Advent wreath around the world and lighting an Advent candle in four different places, leading up to the lighting of the Christmas candle on Christmas morning. The series began in Trinity College, Cambridge with a choir of students who beautifully introduced the Advent hymn 'O come, O come Immanuel' which was to be echoed in all the other places we visited. I interviewed some of the students who spoke about what they saw as signs of hope, living as people of privilege in a world of great poverty.

The second week's visit was in marked contrast when I took the Advent wreath to Zimbabwe. It was not exactly an enjoyable journey, as the BBC, in economy mood, sent me and the camera team by the cheapest possible route on Bulgarian airlines. The journey via Sophia and Lagos took over 24 hours in what I can only describe as Spartan conditions. After an overnight stay in Harare we travelled out to the eastern highlands on the border of Mozambique. We had to drive over perilously rough roads with fascinating rock formations on either side of us. Having survived one burst tyre and one failing clutch, we eventually tramped on foot through deep mud until we reached a circle of thatched huts on the hillsides. There we were welcomed with a joyous hullabaloo from women ululating and children cheering.

In contrast to the cloistered, candle-lit splendour of Trinity College we carried the Advent wreath this time into a dark, thatched African hut, where the only light available was provided by the TV lighting technicians. Then, as one of the young teenagers stepped forward to light the second candle, the people started singing mournfully our theme hymn – O come, O come Immanuel – words in a language they did not understand but expressing a yearning and a hope for freedom with which they could identify.

Much more joyful songs of praise were recorded in the flower-decked Harare Gardens with choirs who had come in from the neighbouring townships and from Harare cathedral. The hymns were accompanied by a Salvation Army band, African drummers and a young people's orchestra. They were sung in English, Ndebele and Shona by turn. The Bible was read by the President of Zimbabwe at that time, the Methodist minister Canaan Banana. I was able to interview him at the Presidential palace. Not long afterwards he was tragically deposed by Robert Mugabe.

The sunlit villages of Zimbabwe seemed a world away from the sprawling housing estates we visited in the north of Edinburgh where we went to light our third Advent candle. But in St Paul's church in Greater Polton there was a faithful remnant of people who were keeping the light of faith and hope burning. I interviewed two women who were doing all they could to persuade young people to turn away from drug addiction and I met with political activists striving to ensure that the community had better facilities and that Edinburgh would have more to boast of than its vaunted festival. The congregation sang not only the Advent hymn as they lit the third candle but also a modern hymn that has since become a favourite of mine, based on the call of the prophet Isaiah, in which the chorus echoes his words in response to God's cry, 'Whom shall I send?' – 'Here I am, Lord. Is it I, Lord?'

For the fourth programme I was able to go back to my beloved Vancouver. There in Stanley Park, against the impressive backdrop of the Vancouver skyline, and among the giant totem poles of the native Canadian tradition, a group of children came singing in procession to light the fourth candle on our Advent wreath. The congregations of several churches had come together in the large St Andrew's Wesley Church, whose ecumenical name signals that it now belongs to the United Church of Canada, where denominational origins are gone but not forgotten. The huge congregation rehearsed and sang lustily for two whole evenings. It's hard work, preparing a programme for *Songs of Praise*! As well as several well known carols the repertoire also included a haunting carol from the native Canadian tradition.

On Christmas morning we returned to Trinity College, Cambridge. Our congregation this time was made up mainly of disabled children who were guests of the community of the college for Christmas Day. The programme included flashbacks to the people we had met over the past four weeks in Cambridge, in Zimbabwe, in Scotland, in Canada and now back in Cambridge. As one of the small disabled children stumbled forward to light the Christmas candle we seemed to be joined with all those friends across the world as we sang together, 'O come all ye faithful – come ye, O come ye to Bethlehem'.

There was one aspect of my radio broadcasting that continued long after I had officially retired from the BBC World Service. Although the religious department at Bush House had come under the independent supervision of the Programmes Editor in the World Service, we had always worked in close co-operation with our colleagues in domestic radio. At that time, it was the custom for the Daily Service on Radio 4 to be led always by members of the BBC staff. Ronald Farrow and I had gone across in turn once a week from Bush House to All Souls', Langham Place (opposite Broadcasting House) to lead the worship, read the prayers (from the BBC book entitled *New Every Morning*) and introduce the hymns and psalms from the BBC hymn book and psalter. The musical director was Barry Rose and the BBC Singers were the choir. The service was broadcast live at 10.45 am leading up to the 11 am news bulletin. I always felt it a privilege to be one of the presenters of this traditional daily service, so I was especially glad to be invited to continue presenting it even after my retirement.

Like so many other radio programmes, through the years the Daily Service underwent many changes to its schedule and its style. The biggest change came when a new controller, David Hatch, was appointed to Radio 4. He introduced radical changes to the whole morning's schedule. He wanted to achieve a seamless effect by allowing each programme on one day of the week to follow on as naturally as possible, focusing on the same theme throughout the day. On this 'Rollercoaster', as it came to be known, no mention was made at first of the place of the Daily Service. So John Newbury, a fellow presenter, and I offered a 'pilot' programme illustrating how we could fit into the new format by presenting an act of worship from a studio, based on the theme for the day and illustrated with recorded music of our own choice. So the new style act of worship was born and has continued on one day of the week ever since, long after the original 'rollercoaster' style of pro-gramming was abandoned.

It was in an act of worship that my attempts to be topical in theme nearly brought me to disaster. It was a Thursday in November 1990 and I recalled that this would be Thanksgiving Day in America, so I decided to take gratitude as my theme and tell the story of the origins of Thanksgiving Day. At 10.42 am while we were waiting to go on the air, Ernie Rae, who was by that time Head of Religious Broadcasting, rushed into the studio to say that there would be a short news flash at 10.45, after which, he suggested, I would need to cut my introduction and go straight into the first hymn. 'What's the news?' I asked. 'Mrs Thatcher has just announced her resignation', he said, 'and what is your hymn?' 'It was going to be "Now thank we all our God!"' I replied.

Fortunately for the sake of BBC impartiality, we were able to substitute from the same CD a more innocuous hymn!

We had reached the end of an era. I wondered what the future held in store for us all.

# 11

# *World of Change*

❧

A s the last decade of the twentieth century approached, the 'winds of change' which Harold Macmillan had spoken about 50 years before took on hurricane force, sweeping across South Africa, the Gulf States and Eastern Europe and resounding through a new developing network of global communication, in a world changing beyond recognition.

For women particularly it was to be a remarkable decade. Impressed by the impact made by the study on the Community of Women and Men in the Church and inspired by the role played by women at the Vancouver Assembly of the World Council of Churches, in 1987 the WCC central committee had resolved that the years from 1988 to 1998 should be observed as a Decade of the Churches in Solidarity with Women. Significantly, the decade was to be launched on Easter Sunday 1988. I suggested to former colleagues in the BBC that this might well be marked by inviting a woman to preach on the broadcast service that Sunday morning, which in those days would still have been unusual. Even in the enlightened circle of the religious broadcasting department I met some reluctance to accept such an idea. It was argued that on this most important festival of the Church year it would be expected that a Church leader such as the Archbishop of Canterbury would proclaim the Easter message, just as the Pope's message to the city and the world is always broadcast at noon on Easter Sunday. I could not resist making the point that the first people ever to proclaim the Easter message were women, even though the men at the time were sceptical.

However, in my own local church a young Caribbean laywoman was invited to preach, and Holy Communion was celebrated by a retired minister, Kathleen Lee, one of the first women to have been ordained in the Methodist Church. After many long years of waiting she had been able to fulfil her vocation and although by this time she was blind she was able to share with us something of what the Easter vision must have meant for those women after the long, sad hours of waiting beside the cross.

At the Lambeth Conference of bishops in that same year, 1988, the concern about the ordination of women to the priesthood was globally the hot topic, threatening to cause division throughout the world-wide Anglican communion. A special commission was appointed under the chairmanship of the Most Revd Robin Eames, the Archbishop of Armagh, to monitor what was happening with regard to this issue in the various Anglican provinces. It was accepted that meanwhile each province would respect the decision of other provinces. In Britain in 1994 the first women were ordained to the Anglican priesthood in a joyous service held in Bristol Cathedral and in many other services in cathedrals throughout the country. By the time of the next Lambeth Conference in 1998, a majority of the Anglican provinces had ordained women to the priesthood and in Canada, New Zealand and the United States a total of 11 women had been consecrated as bishops. In the Church of England, the debate about the consecration of women to the episcopacy continues.

Meanwhile across the world many events were being held not only to celebrate the ministry of women but to express concern about women who were devalued, denied their human rights or degraded as victims of violence at home or in war zones. The important role of religion was emphasized in promoting or preventing the recognition of the God-given dignity of women. A unique Inter-Faith Women's Conference was held in Toronto in June 1988, sponsored jointly by the World Council of Churches' Sub-Unit on Dialogue with Living Faiths, and by the Department on Women in Church and Society.

This conference was remarkable for its style as much as for its content. From the opening moments the atmosphere was informal. Coming from all five continents and six different religious traditions, we met first in the homes of our Canadian hostesses whose hospitality led to immediate exchanges of recipes and chat about our different dietary laws and customs. By the time all 60 participants were assembled in the meeting place we had already exchanged our domestic news, so it seemed natural that our introductions should be personal and anecdotal. Diana Eck, who chaired the conference, encouraged us to share our personal experiences of faith in a world where religious traditions have been mainly shaped by men, though largely preserved and practised by women. There were no main speakers or prepared papers. We were invited in giving our own names to recall also the names of our mothers and if possible of our grandmothers and great grandmothers too. Thus we were reminded of the feminine influences we have inherited, which were often quoted as being the influence of faith, of religious observance and of resilience in face of adversity.

None of the women laid claim to being representative of whole communities or told us what their own professional qualifications were, though we discovered later that there were doctors, journalists, lawyers, pastors, teachers and mothers among us. Each gave her personal story of how her faith allegiance chimed in or clashed with her self-understanding as a woman. Many testified that in the fundamental tenets of their faith they had found affirmation of their female nature, but in the practice of religious institutions they had felt relegated to a subordinate role.

---

For several of the women present, this was their first such encounter. They were aware of the risk involved in stepping beyond the boundaries of their own faith community but they expressed the sense of having a sure enough footing in their own faith to enable them to venture out in exploration of the experiences they shared with women of other faiths. They learned care in the use of language which was challenged whenever it seemed insensitive or ill-defined and many stereotypes were shattered in the impact of face-to-face encounter.

There were some hard days of debate. It seemed that every faith community has its non-negotiable hard core of commitment about which women can be as defensive as men. We realized how religion not only sculpts our cultural identities but can also make us intensely conscious of all that separates us from others. With people there from Israel and the West Bank, from the Sudan and the Punjab, we could not avoid the immediate topical conflicts which for some of the women among us were part of their daily, suffering reality. As we listened to their stories we were made aware of the cost involved in genuine peace-making.

Throughout the dialogue all scriptural exegesis, political analysis, legal explanations, social concerns and personal testimonies were seen through what one woman called 'the restless eyes of twentieth-century women'. We came away from our week together not with recommendations or reports but simply with the resolve to continue the dialogue with our neighbours of other faiths and to develop across the world the many networks through which women learn to communicate with one another in a world still predominantly ruled by men.

Those restless eyes of modern women were alert also at the International Conference of the Council of Christians and Jews which I was invited to address in Montreal in the same year, 1988. A woman rabbi and Hebrew scholar leading our Bible studies encouraged us to consider the stories in the Hebrew Scriptures of some of the hidden, valiant and in some cases abused women who played such a vital role throughout the history of Israel.

On the evening of the Sabbath we were invited to two separate celebrations of this Jewish holy day. One celebration was in the Reformed tradition, a much more informal gathering than the Orthodox celebration to which we were also invited. I found it sad that divisions in the Jewish community are as obvious and apparently as intolerant of one another as they are in the Christian Church. Yet we were welcomed to attend both celebrations.

I had been asked to give a lecture on 'A Christian View of Pluralism'. I argued that it is God's love for us that constrains us to come closer to one another, not our love for God – that fickle, frail sometimes failing love that we hold on to in a godless world where we are all in one sense an alien people, not knowing how to sing the Lord's song in a strange land. Surely, I suggested, the greatest division in our world today ought not to be between those of different faiths but between those who have faith and those who have no faith at all, those who hope and those who despair. Dialogue, like faith, is an affair of the heart rather than of the head, so, like my father in the faith John Wesley, I wanted to quote to those of another faith than mine words from the Hebrew Scriptures (though used in a different context): 'If your heart is as my heart, give me your hand.' I testified to my own non-negotiable commitment to Jesus Christ as my Lord, but I quoted also the title of a book by the Indian theologian M. M. Thomas, my colleague when he was Chairman of the World Council of Churches. He had spoken of 'risking Christ for Christ's sake' and, like him, I felt it no diminishing of my Christian faith to recognize the validity of the faith of others whose love of God took them along different paths of spirituality from mine.

Montreal and Toronto were both as it were stepping stones for me on my way to Vancouver, where I had been invited to spend a term as a Visiting Scholar at the University of British Columbia. I took the opportunity en route of a brief holiday in the company of Margaret Senogles, a friend and frequent companion on overseas travels. We flew up north to the Yukon and to the ramshackle Dawson City, which looked like a deserted film set from a wild west movie. There we attended an unforgettable service in a small chapel on the Sunday morning. A young priest was celebrating his first eucharist. The congregation was made up mainly of Inuit Indians, wrapped in their warm furs, and a few former miners, left behind presumably since the days of the gold rush. Playing the harmonium was 'Diamond Toothed Gertie' who had been billed as the pianist at the casino the night before, and who accompanied one of the miners in a special solo he offered to play in honour of the occasion. We were surprised by his choice of music, which we eventually recognized as Beethoven's Ode to Joy. We were even more surprised by his choice of musical instrument – a set of bag-pipes! A warm welcome was given us as we joined a celebratory party after the service with this simple, sincere and reverent con-gregation.

Coming back to the sophistication and modern developments in the twentieth-century city of Vancouver was a great contrast. I was blessed in being given a flat in the tower of the castle-like building housing the Vancouver School of Theology on the University campus. From my bay windows I had what must be one of the most attractive views in the whole of Vancouver, taking in the sweep of the bay against the backdrop of the mountains. My hosts, who had organized my visit, were the indefatigable June and Len Lythgoe, whose enthusiasm for the ecumenical movement had been fired by their experience in preparing for and participating in the Vancouver Assembly. So June had suggested to the University, though it is a secular institution, that I should be invited to give three major lectures on ecumenism in a specially endowed series known as the Murrin memorial lectures. Under the overall title *Breaking Down Barriers* I described the programmes and studies through which the World Council of Churches aimed to overcome racism, to encourage partnership between women and men in the life of the Church and the community and to facilitate dialogue between peoples of different faiths and ideologies as well as working for unity between the churches. The lectures were well attended and the discussions following them were provocative and lively.

My other major assignment during my term at UBC was to teach a weekly class at the Vancouver School of Theology on the subject of communication, both through the media and in the pulpit. I still believe passionately in the value of preaching, which P. T. Forsyth once described as 'the organised hallelujah of the whole congregation'. Most of the students at VST were preparing for the ordained ministry, so I tried to emphasize in my classes that those who preach regularly to a local congregation, however small, need to exercise the same discipline in preparation and to be as aware of the constraints of time and of context as those who communicate through the mass media. One of the greatest orators of the early Church, Chrysostom (whose name literally means 'golden-mouthed'), once said, 'Preaching is not a natural but an acquired power'. In a teasing paradox he went on to say it was one in which 'the gifted need to take greater pains than the unskilful'.

It was my privilege to share in several services both in local churches and on radio and television during my term in Vancouver. I was particularly glad that I could be present at the launching of the Ecumenical Decade of Churches in Solidarity with Women for the whole of the Vancouver area. It was a most imaginative event and remarkably well attended, despite a down-pour of rain just as we were setting out for the service. The liturgy had been prepared by a local group who made effective use of the images of bread, water, fire and incense as they celebrated the work of women across the world in words and music. One woman had a remarkable gift for telling Bible stories that made us feel as though we were listening to them for the first time. I chose as my text the words of Jesus to his disciples, in the story of the woman who brought perfume as a gift to him: 'Why do you make trouble for the woman?'

For another major event during this 'Women's Decade', in 1989 I went to Kenya at the invitation of the Lutheran World Federation. They were organizing a consultation for women from all over Africa on Women in Media. Its aim was two-fold. The first aim was to alert women to the influence of the mass media at a time when the global communications industry was becoming the fastest growing in the world. It was pointed out that often the remotest villages now had access to transistor radio sets and even video players. Women who had never had the chance to learn to read or write and who still spent up to 18 hours daily fetching water, chopping wood, working in the fields and getting food for the family meal, could now see and hear how the other half of the world lived. They saw women who not only had more leisure but also enjoyed luxuries they themselves had never dreamed of but were tempted to crave. Since most radio, television and film pro-grammes originated in the West, the moral values and social norms and images of women transmitted were those of an alien culture and were often exploitative or sexist.

The second aim was to encourage a greater participation of African women in the control and production of radio, television and other media of communication in their own continent. Several of the women attending the consultation were themselves journalists, some of whom had had the opportunity of training overseas and whom I had met earlier at special courses given by the

BBC. They quoted good examples of the way in which broadcasting was increasingly being used as a means of extending education in Africa and of furthering international understanding. They stressed the need for more locally produced programmes and for making use of native talent and of traditional means of communication.

Within the seminar itself we had extempore dramatic presentations illustrating both the good and bad influences of the media. For example, one group enacted a scene in which a village woman was milking her one cow in order to provide nourishment for her children and at the same time was enjoying listening to the radio. Then she heard a commercial jingle about the delights of a bottle of fizzy drink, so she sold her fresh milk and went off to buy one for her children. When her baby then became ill she heard another advertisement telling her to buy a special baby food, so she was tempted this time to sell the cow also, until at the last moment a local nurse came to dissuade her from paying too much attention to what she heard on the radio!

Some groups worked on developing other, more traditional forms of creative communication. Classes in photography produced an excellently illustrated calendar, and a tie-dyeing session created colourful materials for the latest African fashions.

A leading, talented woman from Kenya, Musimbi Kanyoro, was one of my colleagues as a fellow speaker at the first international congress of the World Association of Christian Communication held later in that same year, 1989. WACC owes its origins to the vision of the ecumenical pioneer and prophetic peace-maker, Bishop George Bell of Chichester. Throughout the Second World War he had worked tirelessly to keep communication open between the churches in nations at war with one another. After the war he had encouraged the Revd Edwin Robertson and the Revd Francis House, both of the BBC, to convene a conference of professional European broadcasters. Coming from ten European countries, they met in Chichester in 1950 and together produced a statement on the aims and methods of Christian broadcasting in a post-war world. This led eventually to the setting up of a World Association for Christian Broadcasting, which later expanded its concerns to include all forms of media and their influence upon society as a whole. Continuing to develop as the World Association for Christian Communication it supported a variety of projects across the world including both print and electronic media.

The first international congress of the WACC, held in Manila in October 1989, took as its theme 'Communication for Community'. The Congress was opened by the new President of the Philippines, Corazon C. Aquino, who, speaking of the recent upheaval in her country, witnessed to the power of the media when she said:

> Our revolution, won by the deepest faith, was a miracle ably supported by Christian communicators, especially the radio broadcasters, who played a key role in mobilizing the people . . . Faith, through people power, overcame the dictator's fire power even as we recognize that it was also a victory of Christian communication.[1]

There was an infectious air of optimism among the young people we met in the Philippines. With their natural love of theatre they retold the history of their country in dramatic sketches. First they had been ruled by the Spaniards, and behaved piously as though they were living in a convent. When the Americans came, their islands became like an outpost of Hollywood. Then the Japanese arrived and the whole area became a battlefield. Following that, they had their own rulers who built luxury hotels and

---

1 Congress opening address quoted in *Media Development* April 1990, p. 40.

paraded the latest fashions. Just two years previously they had discovered what they called People Power, when the young people
thronged into the streets in thousands, armed not with weapons
but with yellow roses and streamers and calling for change, echoing the demands being heard across the world at the same time, in
East Germany, in South Africa, and courageously earlier in the year
even in China.

In the declaration that came out of the 1989 WACC Congress in
Manila it was recognized that the world was at a crucial stage in the
development of the means of communication. The imbalance in
the origin and control of the world's media had been analysed in
detail some years before in the UNESCO Commission for the
Study of Communication which, under the presidency of Sean
MacBride, had issued a report called *Many Voices, One World*. It
called for 'a more just and more efficient world information and
communication order', a call opposed by many Western govern-
ments but supported by most developing countries. The Manila
declaration called on the WACC to formulate a set of common
principles of international communication.

In fact, the world was on the brink of the most extensive of all
developments in the media of communication. In March 1989 a
young man called Tim Berners-Lee published a proposal for a new
form of information management. His boss allowed him to work
on a global hypertext system. A colleague called Robert Cailliau
worked with him on a further development of it and in 1990 they
decided to call it 'the world wide web' and thus brought into being
a whole new global network of electronic communication.

For me, the year 1990 was particularly memorable as among
many return visits to Canada I was invited to address in August of
that year a great ecumenical Christian Festival held in Halifax,
Nova Scotia. There all the churches combined in a three day
event including a procession of witness, a kind of market place

displaying the concerns and activities of various Christian organizations and a marathon of meetings with speakers from all over the world. I was invited to share the platform with Desmond Tutu, now Archbishop of Capetown, and free to travel abroad. His words were full of hope as he spoke of the rapidity with which the situation was changing in South Africa. They stood at last, he said, on the threshold of new possibilities. State President de Klerk had raised the ban on the African National Congress. The whole world had rejoiced when on 11 February Nelson Mandela walked out of prison, free at last after a lifetime's gaol sentence. But there was still a long way to go before South Africa would become a fully democratic country in which Desmond himself would have a right to vote, previously denied to him and to all Africans in South Africa.

Whenever Desmond and I met we always parted with the traditional toast, 'Here's to our next meeting – next year in Johannesburg!' This time that wish came true. Later in that same year 1990, I was invited to be one of a group of four to represent the World Council of Churches at the first Conference of all the South African Churches, including segregated denominations that had upheld apartheid. It was to be held at Rustenburg. So I had to go to the office in South Africa House to request that the ban on my travelling to South Africa be removed and that I be permitted to travel to attend the Churches' Conference. I met with some hesitation but eventually, just two hours before I was due to depart for the airport, I had a phone call telling me to collect the visa from South Africa House, giving me permission to stay in South Africa for one week only. I flew first to Geneva for a brief meeting about a session I had promised to prepare for the Canberra Assembly the next year. Then, almost exactly 20 years after I had been refused permission to enter Johannesburg airport, I arrived there again, this time to join a long queue at the passport desk for a searching interview about my reason for coming and a warning that I must not out-stay the duration of my visa. I eventually was met at the exit and driven to a hotel in the Hillbrow district of the city.

Frank Chikane, who was at that time the General Secretary of the South Africa Council of Churches, came to breakfast with me to explain that the Rustenburg Conference was originally suggested by President de Klerk in his speech on Christmas Day 1989. The churches, preferring not to meet under state auspices, set up their own steering committee, inviting Barney Pityana (a South African Anglican priest who had been living in England) to return from exile and take over the job as organizing secretary. All the churches in South Africa had been invited to send representatives and a few international visitors were expected. The basic issue was no longer apartheid, for it had become generally agreed now that such a doctrine was theologically indefensible. The question at stake was the future relations between churches which for so long had been separated and which could surely only be truly reconciled to one another through some expression of repentance for the past.

After breakfast we left by road for Rustenburg, just under two hours' journey along wide roads leading to a luxurious hotel where we registered for the conference. We were staying in a place called the Wigwam where we had our own individual chalets built along-side an inviting swimming pool. My neighbours were my good friends Aruna Gnanadason from India, secretary at the Women's Desk at the World Council of Churches, and the Revd Oscar McCloud, an African-American Presbyterian who had been a fellow member of the WCC Executive Committee.

The conference began with an exuberant opening service in which Desmond Tutu praised the great 'God of surprises'. Refer-ring to recent events in Eastern Europe as well as in South Africa, he enthused, 'Freedom is breaking out all over the place.' People who were once demonized were now sitting down at the same table to talk to one another. The most extraordinary card God had played was calling all the churches in South Africa to meet together, which itself was nothing short of a miracle!

It was a highly charged meeting with moments of great drama and others of quiet anger and bitterness at the terrible cost that had been paid in human life and suffering. Dr Willie Jonker, Professor of Systematic Theology, speaking on behalf of the NGK (the white *Nederduitse Gereformeerde Kerk*), listed the obstacles that had blocked the way to mutual understanding between the churches, quoting ignorance and a sense of isolation as among the greatest barriers. At the end of a measured, unimpassioned speech, he declared that it was no longer possible to go ahead as if all was well, without acknowledging the wounds and the sins of the past. Then he stunned us into silence as he declared unequivocally, 'I want to confess before you and before the Lord not only my own sin and guilt for the structural wrongs that have been done to you and from which you are still suffering. Vicariously I would like to do that in the name of the Afrikaans people as a whole. I can do that now because the Synod has declared apartheid to be a sin.'

To this speech Desmond Tutu made a swift personal response expressing forgiveness. Some thought the response was maybe too swift. I heard two African ministers sitting behind me saying quietly to one another, 'I shall believe they have changed their minds only when they have changed their actions.' John de Gruchy of the United Congregational Church made a longer response, warning that only a naïve romantic would believe that all the difficulties of the past could be easily overcome. Any talk about reconciliation in South Africa would be cheap unless there was a determination not only to remove the legislation of apartheid but also its legacy.

The next day the Moderator of the NGK made a special statement endorsing unambiguously the stand taken by Professor Jonker. Desmond Tutu called the meeting to a silent prayer of thanksgiving and then repeated on behalf of the whole conference the forgiveness he had expressed the day before, saying 'There are no guarantees in grace. We have to have the vulnerability which Jesus himself showed on the cross.'

In the final declaration from Rustenburg there is a key sentence which reads: 'Some of us are not in full accord with everything said in this conference but on this we are all agreed, the unequivocal rejection of apartheid as sin.'

The day after the conference ended turned out to be one of the most momentous days of my life. I spent the morning trying to get my visa extended and Aruna spent it trying to find a lost case, but after lunch we were offered a run out to Soweto. We arrived at an arts centre in time to hear a string quartet playing Mozart. Immediately following that our driver took us further into Soweto past streets of little houses, some of them shacks, and then uphill to a larger house where we passed through security gates which electronically opened for us. There, to our total amazement, standing at the top of the steps to greet us in person were Nelson and Winnie Mandela! He received us most graciously and ushered us into their tastefully furnished pink and grey lounge. When I commented that he must be feeling tired, having only just returned from a journey to India, he replied with great charm, 'But it's most refreshing to meet people like you!' He told us what it had meant to him in prison to know of the support we were giving him through the Programme to Combat Racism. He asked where I lived and when I replied, 'Wembley', he recalled how he had heard about the great celebration of his 70th birthday that had been held in the Wembley stadium in 1988, the news of which reached him even in his prison cell. I had a camera with me and was almost too shy to ask for a photograph but he willingly suggested that we all went out on the verandah for a group picture. Although this was in the early days of his release, I was aware that we were in the presence of a great statesman, a man of simplicity, sincerity and incomparable strength. As we came away, Oscar commented, 'I feel like Simeon – now let me depart in peace, mine eyes have seen thy salvation!' I knew exactly what he meant.

After all the euphoria of watching such exciting events unfold in the new South Africa the fierce thunderstorms that rocked our plane as we took off for home from Johannesburg airport seemed like an ominous portent of what lay ahead. The newspapers in Britain were full of the gathering threat of what was to become known as Operation Desert Storm.

In August Saddam Hussein's army had invaded and annexed Kuwait, the oil-rich territory to which Iraq had laid claim ever since it was granted independence by Britain in the late 1950s. A coalition of 28 nations were demanding that the Iraqi troops be withdrawn. A UN ultimatum was issued and ignored. On 17 January 1991, the allies began heavy bombing raids lasting over six weeks, followed up by four days' ground fighting which drove back the Iraqi army. In retreat they blew up many of the oil wells. In the aftermath of the fighting were left some two to three million refugees.

This war in the Gulf was barely three weeks old when it was time for delegates to gather for the seventh Assembly of the World Council of Churches scheduled to be held in Canberra, Australia. Some wondered whether the Assembly ought to be postponed at such a critical time. It was argued to the contrary that it was most important that at a time like this Christians from across the world should meet and let their voices be heard, speaking an international message of peace and hope above the sounds of nations at war with one another. When Gabriel Habib, General Secretary of the Middle East Council of Churches, was asked which side he thought God was on in this desert war, he replied, 'God is on the side of the suffering'.

At the pre-Assembly women's meeting it was pointed out that the primary victims of any war are women and children, not only in the areas of conflict but also in the poorer countries of the world whose whole means of livelihood would be affected by the resulting global economic crisis. The women also marked the fact that the Ecumenical Decade of the Churches in Solidarity with Women had been embraced with enthusiasm by women across the world. However it was pointed out that while women welcomed the opportunity to be in solidarity with one another there was not yet enough evidence of the churches as a whole showing the kind of solidarity with women which recognized their gifts and enabled them to participate more fully at all levels of church life. At this Assembly 35 per cent of the elected delegates of member churches were women, only a very small increase on the number who had been present at the Vancouver Assembly.

It seemed to me particularly appropriate that the greatest impact at the Canberra Assembly was made by a woman theologian who had been invited to give one of the major addresses on the theme, 'Come, Holy Spirit – Renew the whole Creation'. It was the first time that an Assembly theme had taken the form of a prayer, and also the first one addressed particularly to the Holy Spirit. So perhaps we ought not to have been surprised that Chung Hyun Kyung, professor of theology at Ewha Women's University, Seoul, set her address in the context of an invocation expressed in word, in symbol and in dance, in which she was accompanied by both Korean and aborigine Australian dancers and drummers. Her presentation was received by some with rapturous applause, and by others in stunned silence! For some people her invocation of the spirits of the departed martyrs of many different cultures and histories was disturbing, and charges of syncretism were laid against her. For others it seemed as though she had been inflamed by the Holy Spirit, that powerful *ruach*, that inspires all truly spiritual strength. A major debate followed her presentation in which the question was raised as to what limits there are to theological diversity. How far is the Church called to Christianize the cultures among which the gospel is preached and how far is Christ to be presented as one who is relevant to all cultures? In a final word in the debate, Professsor Chung warned against Western, male theologians trying to set limits to the Holy Spirit's work. Referring to some of the emerging new theologies, she said, 'Yes, we are dangerous but it is through such danger that the Holy Spirit can renew the church.'

Following this dramatic opening session of the Assembly, I had the awesome responsibility the next day of chairing a round table discussion between well-known figures in the ecumenical movement including Dr Philip Potter, the retired General Secretary of the WCC, a Methodist, Dr Mary Tanner, the ecumenical officer of the Church of England, and Metropolitan John of Pergamon of Turkey, from the Eastern Orthodox Church. Philip emphasized how the Spirit of Truth calls us to transparency in all our dealings with one another not only in our ecclesiastical relationships but also in the economic systems of our global society. Mary spoke of how the Spirit could give us a mobilizing portrait of a visible unity which might well astonish us by its diversity. Authentic diversity would indeed flourish if it were built on the foundation of a rediscovered unanimity in faith expressed in our common baptism, eucharist and ministry. Metropolitan John reminded us that the Holy Spirit does not like to be told what to do, so we must be prepared for the unexpected and work for a spirituality that will make sense for all human beings in all walks of life.

In the resulting discussions throughout the Assembly it became clear that despite the significant theological convergence that had been achieved in recent years the churches were still a long way from achieving that unity which has always been the aim of the ecumenical movement. There were still painful obstacles barring the way to full communion. In an open letter to the Assembly, Orthodox participants insisted that the WCC should make its main aim the restoration of church unity, and that Faith and Order should be given greater prominence in all its deliberations. The Revd Emilio Castro, who had succeeded Philip Potter as General Secretary of the WCC in 1985, commented in his Report to the Assembly

> Although co-operation between the churches is increasing [and he gave many examples of such co-operation], the processes of unity are slowing down . . . It looks as though with the growth of the means of communication and an increasingly conscious option for plurality, our division is more and more accepted as an inevitable fact of life. Not that there is any lack of goodwill for church unity. But there is a lack of ardour and impatience.[2]

The 'Desert Storm' was not the only event which made us aware at Canberra of the winds of change sweeping across the world. I personally was glad of the opportunity to meet again with some of the aborigine friends we had visited ten years before. It was good to see their active participation in the Assembly and to note how some of the Australian Church leaders seemed much more aware of wrongs done in the past and of the need to restore better and more just relationships. Our spirits were lifted too by the enthusiastic singing of a South African choir rejoicing in their newly won freedom. For the first time since leaving the World Council of Churches after the Cottesloe consultation in 1960, members of the (white) Dutch Reformed Church were present among us as observers.

---

2 Quoted in *Signs of the Spirit,* Official Report of Seventh Assembly, WCC, 1991.

One of the greatest moments of the whole Assembly was the reception of the representatives of the Chinese Protestant Churches in mainland China attending an Assembly for the first time in over 30 years. Now collectively known as the China Christian Council and regarded as a united Church rather than a council of churches, they were welcomed back into the membership of the World Council of Churches as the 317th member church. It was particularly moving to see the Revd Chun-Ming Kao, of the Presbyterian Church in Taiwan, embracing Bishop Ting, the President of the Chinese Church, in welcome.

Moments like that are for me what the ecumenical movement is all about – the meeting of people across all the dividing walls, political, racial, cultural or ecclesiastical. The winds of change that were bringing so many walls down during this last decade of the twentieth century seemed like part of God's answer to the prayer which ended the Message from the Canberra Assembly:

> Come Holy Spirit,
> Come, teacher of the humble, judge of the arrogant
> Come, hope of the poor, refreshment of the weary, rescuer of the
>     shipwrecked
> Come most splendid adornment of all living beings,
> The sole salvation of all who are mortal
> Come Holy Spirit, have mercy on us
> Imbue our lowliness with your power.
> Meet our weakness with the fullness of your grace.
> Come Holy Spirit – renew the whole Creation.[3]

---

3  Quoted in *Signs of the Spirit,* Official Report of Seventh Assembly, WCC, 1991.

# 12

# *Journey to Jubilee*

W hile I was in Canberra I was able to keep up my regular broadcasting assignments by courtesy of colleagues in Australian Broadcasting. It seemed strange to be giving a *Pause for Thought* at the end of a day 'down under', knowing that for listeners at home the day would just be starting. I always enjoyed the challenge presented by *Pause for Thought* on BBC Radio 2. It required not only conciseness of content and simplicity of language, which was a good discipline for a seasoned preacher like myself, but also it needed a way of beginning and ending which fitted easily into the style of the presenter of the early morning programme. Both Derek Jameson, the presenter at that time, and Terry Wogan who succeeded him were most co-operative and helped to make the 'God-slot' and me personally fit comfortably into the general flow of the light-hearted banter of their morning show.

I was also in those days a regular contributor to Radio 4's *Thought for the Day* which had a quite different feel about it. It was in danger at times of seeming like an interruption to a fast moving current affairs programme with little apparent relation to anything that had gone before or came after it. Contributors to *Thought for the Day* were encouraged to be as topical as possible in the subject matter on which they chose to reflect theologically. This became of special importance at times of sudden disaster, when the speaker was expected to be able to give some word of comfort or reassurance. I always found that particularly difficult following an account of some natural calamity – earthquake, flood or hurricane, for which no-one could be particularly blamed, and which would normally be described as 'an act of God'.

For example, in June 1991 I had to speak immediately following news of the unexpected, devastating eruption of the volcano on Mount Pinatubo in the Philippines which was spewing fire and burning boulders down on to the surrounding villages, totally destroying them. I knew that to the tribal peoples living in that area it must have seemed like the wrathful revenge of some great dragon. At such a time I almost wished I were an atheist. It would be easier to give way to what Bertrand Russell called 'unyielding despair' than to attempt to 'justify the ways of God'. God is said to have created order out of chaos, and pronounced the universe good. But there are times when it seems that chaos has come again and the so-called ordered universe is shown to be fatally flawed. Yet faith in the ultimate goodness of God is not required to look desperately for the reasons that bad things happen; it must always look hopefully for the good that could possibly result from them. One consequence of any natural disaster is that it should make us all more seriously aware of the world's fragility and more urgently concerned to care compassionately for those who are its immediate victims, often people long neglected on whom for a brief time the focus of the world's attention shines.

More often, the question of topicality presented speakers on *Thought for the Day* with the problem of being both relevant and impartial where political issues were concerned. With events moving rapidly in all parts of the world, it was difficult to keep up with the pace of change. Due to speak on August Bank Holiday 1991, I thought it would be safe and non-political simply to describe how families would be enjoying a carefree day out together. Then suddenly at 5.30 am on the World Service there was a news flash announcing that Mikhail Gorbachev, who had been introducing many reforms into the Soviet Union, had been overthrown in a coup. By the time I reached the *Today* studio I could tell that the whole programme that morning would be focused on Gorbachev and the possible effect of his being overthrown. Fortunately I had with me an old diary in which I had scribbled down some notes I had taken whilst reading Gorbachev's book *Perestroika* where he had written extensively about his views on the importance of 'basing international politics on moral and ethical norms common to all humankind'. He had declared his conviction that 'humanity deserves a better fate than being a hostage to nuclear terror and despair'. Within the few minutes before I was due on the air I strung three such quotations together, saying that ideas such as these were even more powerful than the people who carried them and who, wittingly or unwittingly, often became the instruments of God's purpose in the world. Mikhail Gorbachev, I suggested, might well have been one such instrument. A hasty phone call to the producer of *Thought for the Day* gave me permission to use this revised script. Paddy Ashdown, then leader of the Liberal Party, was in the studio as the only political leader the programme could contact that morning. He asked me how I had managed to do the necessary research so rapidly. I had to admit that it was sheer good fortune, or maybe the work of the Holy Spirit, that I could find such scribbled notes at a few seconds' notice!

An interviewee whom I was interested to meet in the anteroom of the *Today* programme one morning was Andrew Morton, author of a new book about the royal family which was already causing a sensation and promising to be a bestseller. It was entitled *Diana – The True Story*. Its contents came as such a shock to the general public that it was treated at first with great scepticism. I felt almost sorry for the author when I heard him being searchingly questioned by John Humphrys as to his sources and his motives in writing. It was only many years later, after Princess Diana's tragically early death, that the author revealed that Diana herself had been the main source of the material contained in his book. The year of the book's first publication was 1992, a year which was to produce many more stories of unhappiness in royal marriages and was called by the Queen herself her *annus horribilis*.

It seemed at the time as though all the major institutions of British life were in a state of turmoil. The National Theatre produced a trilogy of plays by David Hare reflecting on the effect of these radical changes. The first play, *Racing Demon*, was a gently comic, sad study of the trials of an Anglican vicar trying to work out in a struggling London parish the implications of the new liberal theology which had become the vogue. The second play, *Murmuring Judges*, took a swipe at the legal system, and the third, *Absence of War*, was a thinly disguised attack on the Labour Party, still struggling at this point to get back into power.

One British institution which David Hare did not feature was also undergoing great change. When John Birt became Director General of the BBC in 1992 he introduced far-reaching changes, not all of which were popular with the staff. He developed the concept of an internal market whereby producers could choose between BBC suppliers and outside markets to provide the facilities they required. He also oversaw the beginning of BBC Online and the promotion of the digital services.

A change which affected particularly those of us who were still engaged in religious broadcasting was the relocation in 1993 of the whole Religious Broadcasting Department, for both radio and television, to New Broadcasting House in Manchester. Inevitably this meant more changes to that time-honoured programme, the *Daily Service*. No longer could it come from All Souls Langham Place, where it had virtually built its own studio, and no longer were the

BBC Singers available daily to lead the music. A suitable venue near to Manchester was sought and found at Emmanuel Church, Didsbury, where the staff were most welcoming. A choir of professional singers was recruited locally, and a rota of musical directors was drawn up mainly from choirmasters and organists within the north of England. The practice of using only members of staff as presenters of the service had ceased and people from many parts of the country and from many denominations were drawn into the rota of regular presenters whose voices and variety of styles became familiar to the listeners. For those of us who still lived in the south, leading the Daily Service meant a journey to Manchester and an overnight stay to ensure our being at Didsbury in time for the rehearsal at 8.30 am and for the live transmission at 9.45 am. The tradition of an Act of Worship coming once a week from a studio was continued, and on such days it was still possible to broadcast down the line from a studio in London.

Meanwhile, at weekends I travelled to preaching appointments in many different parts of Britain and went on occasional lecturing tours to the USA and to both the east and west coasts of Canada. In 1997 I celebrated what was for me a most memorable weekend when the Methodist Conference was held in London. It was the year in which Robert Maginley, the teenager I had met by chance in Antigua 20 years before, was due to be ordained. Robert had eventually offered for the ministry while studying in New York. He had then come to Britain in response to an invitation to take part in the Opportunity for Ministry Programme we had launched at Harlesden in the hope of encouraging more black candidates to serve in the ministry here. During the years of his training he had become a kind of 'son in the gospel' to me and so I had been invited to preach at his ordination service which that year was to be held in St Margaret's Church, Westminster. As it happened to be my 70th birthday on the eve of that Sunday, Shirley, Robert's wife, had organized a splendid birthday party for me in no less a place than the Jerusalem Chamber in Westminster Abbey, kindly booked for the occasion by Canon Donald Gray, at that time priest at St Margaret's. It was a thrill to celebrate in that historic place such a landmark occasion, surrounded by friends who had played a part in so many different periods of my life.

I was delighted when the next year I was invited by Stephen Shipley to be one of the leaders of a BBC pilgrimage to the Seven Churches of the Apocalypse. We would be visiting early Christian sites mentioned in the Book of Revelation and would broadcast Daily Services from places where some of the earliest Christian communities once gathered for worship. The pilgrims who came with us would form a volunteer choir. I persuaded my sister Joy to come with me. Unlike me she has a good singing voice and so was able to join the other singers. They worked hard under the baton of Gordon Stewart, a demanding as well as an entertaining conductor, and tackled some ambitious anthems as well as a catholic selection of old and new hymns.

After a crowded day sight-seeing in the bewildering city of Istanbul and a tantalizing glimpse of a few of the 30,000 stalls in the Grand Bazaar, we gathered in the Anglican Chaplaincy for our first recorded service. The preacher was the Anglican chaplain, and fellow presenters Angela Tilby, Oliver McTernan and I shared in leading the service and the intercessions. The next morning we paid a courtesy call to the Patriarchate, the seat of the Ecumenical Patriarch of the Orthodox Church. In the ornate little church, tucked away in a side street of the city, rows of plush seats had been set out in preparation for our arrival. The liturgy was still in progress when we arrived so we had half an hour's peaceful listening time, a welcome and restful contrast to the bustling noise of the previous day's busy schedule. Then Patriarch Bartholomew himself arrived, and to everyone's astonishment, including my own, immediately greeted me personally by name, explaining that we knew one another well through meetings of the World Council of Churches. It was an unexpected but useful demonstration of the friendships forged through the ecumenical movement. In his address to us Patriarch Bartholomew eloquently compared the divided Church to the torn raiment of the body of Christ. As he called us all forward to receive gifts of small crosses, the pilgrims spontaneously began singing, beautifully and hauntingly, 'Come Holy Ghost, our hearts inspire'.

Throughout the rest of our journey we were visiting sites where Christians had worshipped long before there was any division in the Christian Church as it spread across Asia Minor. The journey was not easy because the weather was not good and there were times when we looked and felt like real pilgrims as we paddled across swollen streams or tried to shelter from a heavy downpour. At Laodicea, for example, our Muslim driver valiantly climbed a rock in order to erect a tarpaulin canopy to keep the choir dry. Unfortunately, the canopy itself at times became so flooded that every now and then it tipped its contents over the singers below! As one of the pilgrims commented, 'In the Scriptures the Christians of Laodicea were accused of being neither hot nor cold. We were simply wet through!'

There were high moments of the pilgrimage which we tried to communicate in the services we broadcast. In the huge Roman amphitheatre in Ephesus we vigorously re-enacted the scene where the angry mob tried to drive Paul out of their midst until the town clerk came to his rescue and allowed him to escape. At Miletus it was my turn to be the presenter of the service and I was moved by the way in which one of our choir members read Paul's emotional farewell speech to the elders of Ephesus. Being in the same places where these words were first spoken gave them greater pathos.

The highlight for me was the journey across the sea to Patmos. While my colleagues and the choir were battling with the problems of a recording session made extremely difficult by the presence of large crowds of tourists and noisy motor bikes, I was able to spend some blissfully quiet moments in the cave where it was believed St John had his vision with his scribe sitting beside him writing down the Revelation. It was easy to imagine the apostle looking out of the window over the sea to Ephesus and longing for the heaven in which there would be 'no more sea'.

In Ephesus itself we had been made well aware that we were approaching the end of a millennium. Outside the house where it was reputed the apostle John had brought Mary the Mother of Jesus to live, there were huge signs in a multiplicity of languages inviting people from all over the world to come to Ephesus to celebrate the 2000th anniversary of the coming of Christ. The fascinating thing about the House of Mary was that its walls were placarded with stories of her life, most of them quoted from the Koran, where Mary is honoured in Muslim tradition, as well as in the Christian scriptures.

It seemed as though, as the end of an era drew near, people became ever more fascinated by the past. Pilgrimages became the fashion. On three occasions I was invited to accompany groups of pilgrims from the Vancouver School of Theology, whose Professor of Church History, the Revd Gerald Hobbs, decided that it was more effective to 'walk' history rather than just talk it. So he brought them to Europe where I joined them on three pilgrimages – one to Strasbourg in France, visiting places connected with the Reformation; one to Bedfordshire, Oxford and London, in the footsteps of some of the nonconformists; and one to Dublin in search of the Celtic tradition. Also, as a voluntary job during my retirement, I had become a 'Heritage Steward' at Wesley's Chapel and Museum in City Road, London. There too we received frequent groups of pilgrims from America and many other parts of the world, eager to explore their Methodist heritage.

As the century drew to its close there was an air of apprehension and anticipation everywhere. Despite the ending of the so-called Cold War, the 90s had been a tumultuous decade with its cruel civil wars in Afghanistan and the Balkans, in Sierra Leone, in Sri Lanka and the Sudan and its fearful outbreaks of genocide in Rwanda and in the Congo. But there had also been some signs of hope – peace negotiations, like the Dayton Accord which finally brought to an end the tragic war in the Balkans, the frequent attempts to arrive at a peaceful solution to the age-long conflict in Northern Ireland and the growing concerted concern among churches and other socially committed organizations for a more just global economic order. The advent of the 'New Labour' government of Tony Blair in 1997, elected by a large majority, was greeted with great enthusiasm, and preparations began for the celebration of the dawn of a new millennium.

'Turn to God – Rejoice in Hope' therefore seemed an appropriate theme at the time for the eighth Assembly of the World Council of Churches scheduled to be held in Harare in 1998. Some misgivings had been expressed about the venue, in view of the growing political turmoil within Zimbabwe, but it was decided to keep to the original plan and to make this event an occasion for celebrating the Jubilee of the World Council of Churches itself. I was commissioned, together with John Peterson, a TV producer in the USA, to prepare for the Assembly a large screen video presentation of the history of the WCC from the First Assembly in Amsterdam 1948 up to the present day. This meant hours spent in Geneva looking through archives, photographs and videos of past gatherings and tracing the story unfolding as the Council had grown in a rapidly developing world. At the first Assembly in Amsterdam there were 147 member churches, the majority of whose representatives were male, white, western Church leaders. In Harare, the largest Assembly in WCC history, the 336 member churches were represented by 367 women and 599 men. Just over half these representatives were ordained; the rest were lay people. By their dress and language it was immediately apparent that they came from every continent. In all there was an assembled company of over 1600 including delegates, observers, advisers and staff, plus the greatest number ever of accredited visitors from the whole of Africa as well as from further afield.

For women, the Harare Assembly itself began with a colourful festival celebrating the end of the special Decade of Solidarity with Women. Over a thousand women from all over the world gathered in the Belvedere Technical Teachers' Training College, where our African hostesses gave an enthusiastic welcome to each region of the world separately, expressing in dance and song what they associated with that particular area. So Africans were greeted with drumming, Latin Americans with dance, Asians with eastern music, and, most moving of all, the Middle East was held up before God in fervent prayer for a permanent, just and lasting peace.

Then in a moving, symbolic gesture, women representing all the different nations brought forward containers of water carried from their homelands, and poured them together into a large earthenware pot standing in the centre of the stage. There, mingled together, they represented the shared toil, tears and triumphs of women throughout the world.

At the end of one searing session of testimonies focusing on violence against women, the Korean theologian Chung Kyung Chung lifted our spirits by urging us not simply to weep together but to stand and stretch out our arms, and to recall the gesture of love for all demonstrated by Jesus on the cross.

Among the few men present at the Women's Festival, Konrad Raiser, the current General Secretary of the World Council of

Churches, made a public commitment 'to work for and encourage a community of women and men where the sin of violence against women can be confessed and the healing power of forgiveness can be experienced'.

The exuberance of the Women's Festival somewhat evaporated as we moved over to the campus of Harare University for the full Assembly of the WCC. The weather became wet and cold; deep, mud-filled trenches were cut across the campus and a tropical thunderstorm caused the collapse of the computer system on which for the first time ever an Assembly was depending for its registration process. So the first days were marked by frustration and confusion not only about the physical conditions but also about the disquiet some churches were expressing about the future of the ecumenical movement.

The Orthodox Churches, which had come fully into member- ship of the WCC at the New Delhi Assembly almost 40 years before, were becoming restive. In the post-communist era there had been an influx of sects and other religious movements into Eastern Europe, apparently rivalling long-established Orthodox Christian witness, and tension had also re-emerged between Orthodox and Roman Catholic Churches in the newly indepen- dent states. There was a growing feeling that styles of worship developing at WCC Assemblies and methods of debating and voting were alien to Orthodox tradition. It was reported that the Orthodox Churches of both Georgia and Bulgaria had withdrawn their membership from the World Council. It was agreed that a special commission would be appointed to devote a period of at least three years to studying the full range of issues concerning the continuing participation of Orthodox Churches as a whole in the ecumenical movement.

This was all part of a process that Konrad Raiser described as 'opening up ecumenical space', echoing a phrase used over 25 years before in the statement of the Faith and Order Commission on 'Conciliarity and the Future of the Ecumenical Movement' which had affirmed: 'The church's unity must be of such a kind that there is ample space for diversity and for the open mutual confrontation of differing interests and convictions.' Such a concept had been taken further in a policy statement adopted by the Central Committee in 1997 and commended to the member churches at the Harare Assembly under the title *Towards a Common Understanding and Vision of the WCC.* It envisaged the formation of a forum of churches, which would encompass a fellowship of churches wider than those which felt able to subscribe to the membership of the World Council.

Whilst these dreams of the future were being discussed in the plenary sessions, John Peterson and I were busy rehearsing the presentation in which we would be celebrating the past 50 years of the World Council's life. We had invited as our two major speakers Philip Potter, who had been personally present at every Assembly since the first, and Thabo Mbeki, the new statesman on the scene who had just become President of the Republic of South Africa. Anyone who has ever had to organize an important presentation will know how we felt when, on the very eve of the event, we received a message to say that Thabo Mbeki would be unable to make it. But imagine the relief when we were told immediately afterwards that Nelson Mandela had offered to come as his substitute! Never was a substitute more jubilantly welcomed.

So, just seven years after he stood on the steps of his home in Soweto to welcome those of us who had at last been able to come to South Africa as representatives of the WCC, now I was standing on the steps of the large hall in Harare University waiting to welcome the man universally acknowledged as one of the great statesmen of the twentieth century, Nelson Mandela. Accompanied by the harmoniously singing Milonji Kantu Choral Society of South

Africa, he came up on to the stage, where for a few moments he joined in a dance of joy before I invited him to address us, as one who reminded us that dreams do come true.

> My generation is the product of church education. I recognize that I will never have sufficient words to thank the missionaries for what they did for us. But you have to have been in an apartheid prison in South Africa to appreciate the further importance of the church. They tried to isolate us completely from the outside . . . The link was religious organisations, Christians, Muslims, Hindus and members of the Jewish faith. They were the faithful who inspired us. The WCC's support exemplified in the most concrete way the contribution that religion has made to our liberation.[1]

It was difficult to follow such a moment as Nelson Mandela's entrance and rapturous reception by the Assembly, but there was another magic moment to come. This was when an attractive Zimbabwean teenager came on to the stage to greet Philip Potter, asking him, 'Remember me?' She was the baby who had been brought by her mother, Sithembiso Nyoni, to the Vancouver Assembly and in the opening worship there had been placed in Philip's arms as a symbol of new life. Now Philip challenged 15-year-old Mvuselelo, along with all the youth participants, to look forward to the next jubilee of the ecumenical movement in 2048 as a time when they would be able to testify to what God had done through their generation to carry out God's purpose of good for all.

*Jubilee* was a word that was coming to have significance far beyond the circle of the WCC. In the Hebrew Scriptures the time of Jubilee was associated with a call to release people from their debts. Many churches and other religious groups, relief agencies and

---

1 Nelson Mandela's address to the WCC, quoted in *Together on the Way – Report of the Eighth Assembly of the WCC*, p. 228.

non-governmental organizations celebrated the turn of the century as a time of Jubilee, calling on the richer nations of the world to release the poorer nations from the crippling debts that had been accrued during the time when Western nations had been all too ready to loan, on their own terms, massive sums of money to the developing world.

At Harare on one day the whole Assembly surrounded the meeting hall with one great chain and chanted the slogan, 'Release the chains of debt'. Such protests were to become familiar to many of us over the next few years as we wore the small broken chains that symbolized our support of Christian Aid and the Jubilee movement. The movement's partial success, when some of the worst debts were relieved, led to an even more far-reaching campaign for economic justice and fairer terms of trade. This campaign was also championed by the churches, and attracted secular and celebrity support, taking into the next century the slogan 'Make Poverty History'.

When the new millennium eventually dawned there seemed to be a jinx on most of the plans for celebration. One friend enquired of an officer at London Transport what special public transport arrangements there would be for that new year's eve. He replied, 'I'm not sure. Does anyone know what we did at the time of the last millennium?' Presumably that was why no-one seemed sure how to mark the passing of a thousand years. There was confusion over the distribution of tickets for the great party at the Dome; the millennium bridge turned out to be wobbly, and the planned firework display along the river Thames didn't go off properly. Perhaps these were all portents of far more tragic mishaps to follow.

There was one event that worthily and memorably celebrated 2000 years of Christian art. A special exhibition was mounted at the National Gallery in London, called *Seeing Salvation*. I took a special interest in this as it was sponsored by Jerusalem Productions of which I was by this time privileged to be a director. This was a company that had sprung from a small group many years before called Christians in Media, where our aim had been to encourage sponsorship of religious programmes on radio and television as well as in other forms of media. Eventually known as Jerusalem Productions, we became linked to the Jerusalem Trust which through the Sainsbury charities makes generous funds available for special projects in the media, in education and in social services. The Director of the National Gallery at that time, Neil McGregor, came to discuss with us his idea for an exhibition of paintings of Christ throughout the ages to mark the millennium. It was a hugely successful exhibition supported by lectures and by a superb television documentary. The films shot for television not only of the paintings in the exhibition but of the mosaics at Ravenna and other centres of Christian art so whetted the appetite of my former tutor, and by this time close friend, Doreen Forsyth and myself that, under the leadership of Anglican priest and art expert the Revd Charles Pickstone, we organized an ecumenical pilgrimage to Ravenna which was such an inspiration that we have organized similar art-oriented pilgrimages several times since.

There was one other memorable pilgrimage which for me most effectively marked the beginning of the new era. It was undertaken by a group of us from my local multiracial church in Harlesden, led by our minister the Revd Peter Lemmon. Following a tradition of an annual church holiday to places of spiritual significance, in the year 2000 we were able at last to visit South Africa as a group of black and white friends travelling together. We journeyed under the auspices of Rainbow Tours, a post-apartheid travel agency based appropriately at Canon Collins House and now encouraging tourism to the country which we had for so many years so strenuously boycotted.

We had our share of scenic delights as we soared up in cable cars to the top of Table Mountain, drove around the Cape Peninsula, enjoyed the exotic plants in the Kirstenbosch Gardens and spent a whole morning in the Shamwari Game Reserve of *Born Free* fame. For me personally it was a special joy to be able to visit once more Ilse and Beyers Naudé who had shown me such gracious hospitality during my truncated visit to South Africa 30 years before. Now living in retirement in a delightful cottage in Elm Park village in a suburb of Johannesburg, they were enjoying tranquillity at home and the respect of both the Church and the nation after a life of turmoil and commitment to the struggle for justice.

Like all pilgrimages, this one had its special shrines, among them Robben Island where Nelson Mandela and his comrades had been imprisoned for so long. Almost more moving, because hidden away, was a simple grave at the back of a quiet cemetery near Bisho where Steve Biko lies buried, the young man who did so much to raise black consciousness and who died as a result of torture in a South African gaol. On the wall near his grave was a quotation from his own words, 'It is better to die for an idea that will live than to live for an idea that will die.'

Those words recalled for me some words from David Hare's play *Absence of War*: 'Doing good is easy. The world needs people who will fight evil as well. And that's a much dirtier business.' In these first years of the new millennium there's been plenty of evidence of evil as it has carried terror through the skies, lurked through the streets and spread its poison of fear and hatred. And the world still has not found the right weapons with which to fight it – not the weapons of equally mass destruction, but the weapons of reconstruction, reconciliation and mutual respect that could help to transform our world.

The Harare Assembly had launched a new ecumenical decade –

The Decade to Overcome Violence: Churches seeking Reconciliation and Peace 2001–2010. Ironically, so far this century seems to have unleashed a new kind of violence, the violence of terrorism and the counter-attacks provoked by it.

In this year 2006 the World Council of Churches has held its 9th Assembly, at Porto Alegre in Brazil with the theme, 'God, in your grace, transform the world'. It was a smaller and shorter gathering than in previous years. Sadly I was not fit enough to undertake the long journey to attend it even as a visitor. I would particularly like to have been there to greet the new General Secretary, the Revd Sam Kobia, a minister from the Methodist Church in Kenya. Once Kenya was a small district of British Methodist missions overseas but it has grown into a strong church at whose autonomy celebrations I was present almost 40 years ago. Now, one of that church's sons has become the first member of an African church and the third Methodist to become General Secretary of the World Council of Churches.

Thanks to the real 'world-wide web' I was able to watch the Assembly proceedings daily in my own home, for this web has made the global local as never before. I could join in the enthusiastic, Latin American style of worship and listen to the General Secretary's address. He shared with us his vision for the much larger ecumenical movement which would not be limited to membership of the WCC. He said the central question of our time was the ability to recognize 'the presence of Christ in the other'. He called for the ecumenical movement to be grounded in spirituality, taking young people seriously and working for the kind of global justice that could transform the world in counteracting violence, poverty and disease. He reported how the churches were working together in response to the scourge of HIV and AIDS in Africa. He emphasized climate change as arguably the most severe threat confronting the whole of humanity and urged

Christian churches to speak to the world with one voice on this issue.

I was also able to listen in on the Internet to some of the debates. I found it interesting to note how, in response to the new ways of working proposed by the commission arising from the concerns of the Orthodox Churches, the constitution and rules of the WCC had been substantially revised so as to move to a method of decision making based on consensus rather than on Western parliamentary procedures.

It was disappointing that apart from the coverage on the web, the Assembly seemed to attract in this part of the world much less attention even in the religious press than I had been used to expecting at WCC events. I wondered whether this indicated that the search for ecclesiastical unity, once the apparent priority of the ecumenical movement, no longer seemed such an urgent issue even to the churches. In many ways, despite new divisions threatening within the denominations, relations between the different churches seem so much better now than they once were, and indeed, as one veteran ecumenist, Francis House, expressed it to me in a letter, 'Fifty years of patient work by the Faith and Order Commission have demonstrated that the divided churches agree on basic Christian fundamentals far more substantially than most people realise.'

It used to be argued that the churches could find unity in action even without unity of doctrine. Today it sometimes seems that the reverse is true. Our unity is most threatened when we differ not about doctrine but about the action we should take in applying our faith to the new situations and the ethical dilemmas we are confronted by in modern society. In the context of the present war in Iraq, for example, it seems that Christians are as divided as ever on whether it is possible to agree on what constitutes a 'just war', if such a concept is even still feasible.

---

At Porte Alegro Assembly the mid-term of the Decade to overcome Violence was celebrated with a peace vigil. Never has such a focus seemed more relevant than it does in these early, violent years of the twenty-first century. Now the call must be made to all people of faith to work together for peace between the religions without which there can surely be no peace between the nations. The search for the unity of the Church must always be set within this wider context of the search for the unity of all humanity.

It appears that most institutions that survive beyond their golden jubilee need a fresh injection of inspiration in meeting a changed world situation. The pioneers of the WCC had vision that could see beyond the dark days of the Second World War the possibility of a new ecumenical movement bestriding the national boundaries and denominational histories. They inspired a younger generation which built on the foundations they laid. But as those generations passed on there came a need for new visionaries, new dreams, new structures. I saw a similar pattern in my own church. The Methodist Association of Youth Clubs which was such a dynamic force in my teenage years no longer has much of a constituency left. A new initiative is needed to capture the vision of today's younger generation. We have seen the same process taking place in the United Nations Organisation, launched with such hope and vision at Westminster Central Hall 60 years ago but embroiled in so many conflicts and disputes since that it needs to inspire a new sense of commitment especially from the more powerful nations in the world. I count myself fortunate to have been one of the generation who inherited great visions from the past, but I wonder what form those visions will take in the future.

# Epilogue
## In the Departure Lounge

❧

As I entered upon my 80th year a slightly older friend sent me one of those would-be amusing cards saying, 'Welcome to the departure lounge!' I thought it was not a bad metaphor as a description of old age. I am very familiar with departure lounges where I have waited many hours returning from long journeys. I find that a departure lounge is usually an enjoyable place to be in. It's entertaining to watch the comings and goings, though I confess that now there sometimes seem to be too many 'goings' for my liking. Friends you have been with for a long time go off at their appointed moment, never to return. Meanwhile you have plenty of time and opportunity to meet and talk with other companions around you and to share memories of past journeys and adventures. Usually there are ways of contacting people by phone if you need to, and often a television set by which you can be informed or entertained. You can even have spells of uninterrupted reading. Just occasionally there's a nagging anxiety about when you will actually be called to depart, but most of the time waiting can be in itself a good experience. You have laid down your major responsibilities, you have no more deadlines to worry about and you can trust the Lord to keep you in perfect peace as you learn perhaps for the first time the art of patience. Not knowing what lies ahead, you can savour each present moment for its own worth.

Sharing a birthday with John Wesley as I do has given me the habit in these later years of looking up the birthday entries in his

---

journal as he himself entered upon old age. He made a practice each year of doing a personal check on his state of health both mentally and physically. In his precise, simple use of words he describes so effectively how old age creeps up on us. I quoted his last journal entries in the final broadcast I did for the BBC before totally retiring. It was appropriately in a morning service broadcast from Wesley's Chapel on 29 May 2005. On 28 June 1788 John Wesley wrote:

I this day enter my eighty fifth year. And what cause I have to praise God, as for a thousand spiritual blessings, so for bodily blessings also! It is true that I am not as agile as I was in times past, I do not walk as fast as I did; my sight is a little decayed; my left eye is grown dim and hardly serves me to read. I find likewise some decay in my memory in regard to names and things lately passed, but not at all with regard to what I have read or heard twenty, forty or sixty years ago; neither do I find any decay in my hearing, smell, taste or appetite (though I want but a third part of the food I did once); and I am not conscious of any decay in writing sermons, which I do as readily and I believe as correctly as ever.

Two years later, on 18 June 1790 he writes:

For above eighty six years I found none of the infirmities of old age. But last August I found almost a sudden change. My eyes were so dim that no glasses would help me. My strength likewise now quite probably will not return in this world.

So in the end old age came suddenly to John Wesley as it seems to do to those of us who have been fortunate enough to enjoy good health throughout most of our lives. We know we must eventually lay down many of our former tasks and wait patiently until the departure time arrives. I am confident that when that time does come I who have journeyed all over the world will feel as I did at the end of every long journey, 'How good it is to be going home!'

# Index of Names